POLITICAL
INTROVERTS

To Kelli,

It's been so great getting to Know you.

Keep it up!

Best,

POLITICAL
INTROVERTS

HOW EMPATHETIC VOTERS CAN
HELP SAVE AMERICAN POLITICS

Arthur Lieber

Columbus, Ohio

Political Introverts: How Empathetic Voters Can Help Save American

Politics

Published by Gatekeeper Press

2167 Stringtown Rd, Suite 109

Columbus, OH 43123-2989

www.GatekeeperPress.com

The cover design, interior formatting, typesetting, and editorial work for this book are entirely the product of the author. Gatekeeper Press did not participate in and is not responsible for any aspect of these elements.

ISBN (paperback): 9781642378023

eISBN: 9781642378030

DEDICATION

To every Political Introvert who would like to actively participate in American politics but feels that the system does not welcome them.

To every candidate who runs for political office without bragging, and money-grubbing, but with empathy and critical thinking.

To every teacher who ignores ridiculous expectations from bureaucrats and relates to students with empathy and critical thinking.

To seventeen-year-old Swedish activist Greta Thunberg who models how introverts can honorably effect monumental social change.

PREFACE

Donald Trump is not a political introvert but he is omnipresent in this book. His ascendency to the presidency of the United States is one of the key reasons why we hope that new ways can be found for political introverts to become more engaged and to move us from circus to consensus.

As this book goes to press, Trump has been impeached by the House of Representatives and a trial in the Senate is impending. When you, the reader, glance upon these pages, the status of Donald Trump may have changed considerably. But the points in this book that are made about Trump, and the impact he has on our political process hold true. Our goal is for political introverts to be part of the post-Trump healing process.

TESTIMONIALS

"Count on Arthur Lieber for the freshest insights into our political ecosystem. In Political Introverts, Lieber addresses an urgent question: why are 90 million people not voting? Apathy? Ignorance? A feeling of disempowerment? Lieber posits a different answer: reticence. Citizens might engage in our political system if they were actually welcomed into it. If the value of winning at any cost were tempered with empathy, critical thinking and political literacy about how the system actually works, people might feel ENCOURAGED to participate. The solutions offered: reform of both our educational and political systems, are ambitious, but the present crisis requires exactly this kind of bold challenge."

Rocco Landesman, Broadway producer and former Chairman of the National Endowment for the Arts.

"Arthur Lieber is a one-of-a-kind thinker, teacher, humorist, politically-and-baseball-addicted visionary who is also grounded in facts, creative thinking and practical ideas.

Arthur puts all of the above together in his new book, Political Introverts. He combines his passion and experience in politics and education to provide a starting blueprint to guide our country and its political system into a more empathetic and functional entity."

Andy Rothschild, Former Teacher and Current Artist

"Lieber introduces the concept of the political introvert and argues that it is critical for the success of our participatory democracy that we reclaim a collective identity and humanity around our shared civic experience. Through teaching empathy, Lieber argues we can empower the ordinary citizen to achieve extraordinary civic service."

Dr. Betsy Sinclair, Professor of Political Science; Washington University in St. Louis

In Political Introverts: How Empathetic Voters Can Help Save America Politics, Arthur Lieber's compassion towards disempowered Americans is only matched by his frustration with how Democrats and Republicans have not figured out how to get our system to work. The book is full of intriguing suggestions to bring improvements in both the short-run and long-term.

Ray Hartmann, founder, *Riverfront Times* in St. Louis, MO and Co-Founder & Panelist on PBS-St. Louis Donnybrook

TABLE OF CONTENTS

INTRODUCTION

I F YOU ARE an adult and you did not vote in the 2016 presidential election, you are not alone. There were another ninety-two million of you. That's enough non-voters in the U.S. to include *everyone* in *the eleven largest metropolitan areas* of the country: New York, Los Angeles, Chicago, Dallas, Houston, Washington, DC, Miami, Philadelphia, Atlanta, Boston, and Phoenix. What kind of country would it be if that many people could not vote? Perhaps it would be a country that would select the likes of Donald Trump to be its president, because that's what happened.

In this book, I will look at a subset of the ninety-two million non-voters, those who I'll refer to as **political introverts**. What do I mean by political introvert? I mean people who are not enthusiastic about politics but feel some sort of responsibility to participate in the process. This is not a monolithic group; some are introverted throughout their lives, while others are extroverted in most areas of their lives. While a disproportionate number of political introverts do not vote in elections, many reluctantly cast ballots. The common denominator among them is that they are not happy campers when it comes to politics.

What qualifies me to write this book? Likely the biggest reason is that I consider myself to be a political introvert: aka "P.I." I'm also a political junkie.

I have engaged in the political process by running for Congress twice (I did not win but took the risk of running when no other

Democrat would and was also able to raise many of the points included in this book) and have written for a political blog for ten years. I also have been a teacher for forty years. During fifteen of those years, I co-founded and directed an independent secondary school in St. Louis. My many years working for and with schools have given me insight into the fundamental role schools can and should play in changing our political system.

The introvert in me responds positively to less than one percent of the political stimuli that I receive. But because of my "political addiction," I'm unlike many P.I.s in that I am willing to search for lesser known candidates who match my values. Most political introverts appreciably give up before they seek and find a candidate who doesn't brag, doesn't ask for money, doesn't yell, and has policies that reflect empathy.

Most voters accept the common techniques that candidates use to enlist political enthusiasm such as speeches characterized by pontification, demonizing opponents, and simplifying issues. This doesn't work for political introverts. Neither do the politics of intrusion such as door-to-door canvassing or phone calls. In fact, these standard aggressive tactics often turn political introverts off to the point of disengagement. In this book, we will look at alternative techniques to appeal to political introverts and ideally increase their participation in the political process. This is important if we want to change the results we saw in the 2016 election. I believe the alternative techniques also will elevate American conversations about politics.

If you are an operative for the Democratic or a Republican Party, you tend to salivate when you see statistics like ninety-two million not voting. Each side is consistently looking for ways to bring new voters into its political tent while retaining the base that it has already established. The effort is designed to try to construct a winning coalition. Politics is a "win-lose" game.

But is there a "greater good" for the nation that transcends political parties winning elections? Is there a way in which we can bring those currently disenfranchised or disinterested voters into the political process?

My desire is for our political system to serve the American people—to use our political system as a tool to become a better society. Many observers believe that current politics does not provide realistic ways to express compassion. If we are going to reach the point that we no longer elect Donald Trump-type candidates, we must have an electorate composed of better critical thinkers who have an empathetic concern for promoting the common good of all.

There are two reasons why I wrote this book. First, to help shine light on the need for more empathy in our society and thus in government. Second, to help find ways to attract current non-voters, particularly those who are empathetic and/or introverted, to the voting process, specifically by suggesting changes to our political process that will make the system less repelling to them.

In the preparation of this book, I have conducted surveys and questioned a focus group of non-voters to try to learn more about who they are and what might get them to vote. Do they choose not to vote because of the candidates they see on the ballots? Is the process of voting a turn-off? Do they simply think that their vote doesn't matter? Or is it all too complicated, too difficult to get helpful information to make wise decisions?

Finally, is it simply apathy? There are still millions of potential voters who, when asked their opinion about a political issue say, "I don't know, and I don't care." Not knowing or caring may seem innocuous, but when forty percent of the adult population does not vote in the presidential election, these non-voters have one thing in common. They have forfeited their right to be part of the solutions to our problems.

If our goal is to bring more empathetic people into the voting ranks, we do so at a time when each of the two major political parties in the United States has constructed roadblocks to candidates and policies that can lead us to empathic outcomes. Clearly, Republicans are much more obstructionist than Democrats, for decades they have been the power behind the gridlock in Congress. But we can't let Democrats off the hook. Some Democrats prefer the safety and security of their professional jobs to concern themselves too deeply with people whose rights are being abused and with folks with less privilege than themselves.

Our body of knowledge about why people belong to one party or another is constantly growing. The reasons are not limited to socio-economic status or the influences parents have on their children. We now know that the characteristics of members of each party can be related to the genetic make-up of people who identify with each party[1]. Some people's brains are wired for them to be more empathetic and open to new experiences, and they tend to vote Democratic. Some prefer structure and order, and they tend to vote Republican.

---

1   https://www.npr.org/templates/transcript/transcript.php?storyId=724999235

Regrettably, the political landscape is filled with many Republicans who don't mind being callous. They often act like takers, not givers. If low - and middle-income Americans do not have access to affordable and comprehensive health care, Republican politicians seem content to further limit their access by not requiring that all citizens have a health care plan in which pre-existing conditions are not deal-breakers on insurance coverage.

But Democrats also have their blind spots when it comes to empathy. "Liberal" colleges and universities, which are supposed to be citadels of reason, are often devoid of empathy towards students. They frequently fail to recognize the inherent imbalance of power under which students live and work, all while operating in a system that is striving primarily for money and status. Too often students are treated with little respect. The price we pay as a society is not just the opportunity costs associated with fewer college graduates. The cost includes the mental torment that many students, and even faculty, endure due to the stresses of the university environment.

The backbone of the Democratic Party is now made up of individuals who work in our most prestigious professions. These specialties include doctors, lawyers, academics, financial planners, artists, philanthropists, software engineers, and numerous skilled workers in government agencies. But the road to entry into these professions is often difficult to travel. What high-paying job is accessible without jumping through hoops to gain accreditation and certification? Sometimes the rules to gain credentials make sense. That would be true for surgeons or engineers. Other times the reasoning for complicated certification is questionable at best, as with a cinematographer or even a school teacher. It has become far more difficult to become a self-taught professional. Democrats like it this way in order to increase the status, exclusivity, and power of many of its members.

The two parties being as they are, what strategies can we adopt to bring more empathy into our society? The answer may be surprising. The greatest impediment to making our society more caring, responsive, responsible, and empathetic **is the tight bureaucracy that now has a stranglehold on our nation's public schools.** This situation cannot be pinned on Republicans. Democrats and their close political allies, including the education bureaucracies that grew as Democrats placed more top-down mandates on schools, are primarily responsible. The major impact of these new laws and regulations were to put schools into straight-jackets and eliminate most opportunities for creativity and spontaneity. The intentions may have been good, such as providing more services for under-achieving students, but the methods used often tied the hands of those at the grassroots level, the teachers.

Getting schools to change is a long-term project. Politicians look for quick fixes. Most voters are members of the "short attention span theater audience," and have difficulty dealing with either complexity or patience. Fear is an emotion that generates quick responses, and Republicans have been very skillful in using that as a motivator to get voters to side with them.

Reforming politics is also a long-term project. The strategy will have to be visionary and the tactics will have to be designed to consistently move us forward. We can no longer afford the "one step ahead and two steps back" approach. Hopefully when we revisit our political system in thirty years, we will have made positive strides towards developing more responsive leaders and a more engaged electorate.

A key component to effecting these changes is increasing the amount of empathy in our society. We need to do better at feeling the pain of others who are suffering, and also recognize that as we address problems, we are all limited in what we can do. We are "works in progress" and must have humility. We should view our actions with a sense of irony and recognize that what we do and how we act either is or can seem to be absurd. In an existential world, this is often the best we can do.

In recent years, there has been increased fascination with the Myers-Briggs test, which in part can tell us where we fit on the introvert-extrovert scale. Most of us fit in the middle, an area described as ambiverts.

My quest to provide awareness and motivation to political introverts led me to create seven key points that I offer in this book. These points either level the playing field for introverts, or represent key ways in which political introverts can improve our political system to benefit all of us.

We must make politics friendlier for political introverts. Political introverts need to be allowed to engage in politics without being part of the circus that surrounds it. They need to be able to receive information about candidates and issues from new media outlets, ones that can be trusted and will be capable of individualizing. Political introverts need to be valued, and even catered to, by all candidates, whether those candidates are introverted or extroverted.

All voters need to refine and utilize their B.S. detectors when

it comes to politics. There seems to be an inverse relationship between age and ability to detect when someone is bullshitting. We need to have today's youth take today's adults back to the time when they were young and could better tell when someone was playing them as a fool, be that a teacher, a politician, or anyone else. We need to hold authority figures and the media responsible for breaches of integrity and demand truthful coverage and reporting.

More citizens need to take the risk of becoming political candidates. There are three key reasons why many qualified people do not run for office: (a) they don't think that they can win; (b) they believe they have to raise impossible amounts of money; and (c) they are repulsed by the current political atmosphere and would sooner get elective surgery than subject themselves or their families to such a process. Counter to Vince Lombardi and all the macho coaches' mantras, winning is not everything, or more specifically, there is more than one way to win. Running an honorable campaign and raising important issues is the kind of win America needs most. As for the money, why should candidates bust their butts and compromise their ethics to raise a ton of it. Campaigns today can be cheaper than ever with utilizing the internet and the media's free publicity. All of us need to put pressure on media outlets to identify this new breed of thoughtful, low-keyed, low-budget candidates and to pay proper attention to how they are working to change politics and American life.

Gently encourage people who are not voting to consider doing so. Most non-voters have good reasons, at least in their own minds, as to why they do not vote, and most don't change their voting behavior after being screamed at or beaten over the head with guilt. Many have become locked into not voting and have spent years justifying why they don't. They need to be treated with empathy, not harshness. Many have been oppressed or suppressed by circumstances beyond their control and/or the system in general. We need to seek to understand and provide a hand over the barriers so that our important group of political introverts votes in 2020. We need to find ways to make it easier for non-voters to (a) vote, and (b) find candidates to their liking.

Reduce the shameful presence of large and mysterious sums of money in politics. The amount of money in political campaigns is unfathomable to many and offensive to those who prefer to live within their means. We need to track the dark money in politics, and if we can't determine from where it comes, we need to at least make public which candidates are receiving it. While there are remarkable groups like OpenSecrets.org that are doing their best to find the sources of these dollars, much slips under the radar. With renewed engagement by the media, we need to inform voters about the size and general source of donations for all political candidates for major offices. Most importantly, we need to honor those candidates who run low-budget campaigns.

There is no way that America can reform politics without the help of the media. The current lame-stream media, primarily local television news, is largely disinterested in politics, except when there is scandal. The newest forms of media like social media, cover politics, but are subject to distortion from various nefarious sources including foreign powers. In this book, we will propose new outlets for objective and informative news, funded through charitable contributions. There have to be free outlets for the public to learn about candidates and issues.

Americans need to develop means of assessing politicians by utilizing standards that we would apply to friends and others with whom we hold in high regard. Too frequently in American history, voters have become distracted and turned against the very elected officials who treated them with respect and dignity. It is outright insulting that in the final days of Barack Obama's presidency, the country elected Donald Trump to fill his shoes. We need to ride the positive momentum created every time an honorable official such as Barack Obama runs for office, and wins! To those people who did not vote for Hillary Clinton in 2016 (and indeed it was difficult for some to do so), we must remember how it was obvious that a Trump victory would tarnish Obama's legacy and undo much of his fine work. I am not asking for pity for Obama or anyone else, but we need to show appreciation for those who served with "we the people" in mind and who want to be part of ongoing societal progress in America. Just as we are cautious about turning against personal friends, we need to stay with leaders who have done little to cause us to be turncoats.

Many ideas in this book require risk-taking. Some proposals may push the wrong button for you. But efforts to maintain the *status quo* have left us with Trump. The first step to meaningful change is trial and error. Some of the proposed ideas will stand the test of experience, others won't. We will never find out without trying.

Chapter 1
THE NEED FOR EMPATHY

HERE WAS A genuine a dichotomy in the way in which America's fortieth president, Ronald Reagan, exhibited empathy. It is said that if he was walking along Pennsylvania Avenue outside the White House and a homeless man came up to him and said, "Buddy, can you spare me a dime?" he would reach into his pocket and give the man a dime with good tidings. But if Reagan was inside the White House and a proposal came across his desk to address issues of poverty in the United States, he would reject it as wasteful.

Empathy is a tricky quality. Perhaps this is because the English-speaking world got a late start on the use of the term. In fact, empathy did not appear in the English language until the year 1909[2]. Many reformers think that a lack of empathy is central to what is currently wrong with the American political system. Empathy is fundamental to making our political system more inclusive and responsive to the needs of the electorate.

What exactly is empathy? According to the Miriam-Webster dictionary, it is "the action of understanding, being aware of, being sensitive to, and vicariously experiencing the feelings, thoughts, and experience of another." We know that people who are introverts

---

2   http://www.branchcollective.org/?ps_articles=rae-greiner-1909-the-introduction-of-the-word-empathy-into-english

are more likely to score high in empathy rankings[3]. Many political introverts shy away from politics because empathy is an afterthought to winning the race.

Let's not confuse empathy with sympathy—there is a clear distinction between the two. Sympathy is feeling compassion, sorrow, or pity for the hardships that another person encounters. Empathy is putting yourself in the shoes of another, imagining yourself in the position of someone else who is suffering.

It can be a leap for some people to be empathetic when viewing politics and public policy because the political arena generally does not include people who they personally know. As might have been the case with Ronald Reagan, an individual may have great compassion for someone who they know who is poor. However, this person may not be emotionally aroused by the existence of poverty across America and the world. It's no small wonder that poverty is still so rampant in the U.S.

Some people find it impossible to feel empathy for someone whose life events they have never experienced. Some people are so "empathy-impaired" they feel little compassion even for people they know.

Suppose that you went to the doctor to be treated for headaches you are having. As always, when you go to the doctor's office you are greeted by the admittance clerk or receptionist. She asks you to show her your insurance card and you do. She sees that your insurance company does not cover complications that result from pre-existing conditions. She then looks up your medical history and

---

3   https://www.psychologytoday.com/us/blog/nurturing-self-compassion/201706/seven-reasons-be-proud-be-introvert

sees that when you were in high school you suffered a concussion when playing soccer. She says to you that she doubts the insurance company will cover your current headaches because they probably come from the pre-existing condition of the earlier concussion. But she's nice, so she calls the insurance company to check. After a forty-five-minute wait, she gets a response. You are not eligible for coverage because you had a pre-existing condition.

This is the way insurance companies operated for decades prior to the passage of the Affordable Care Act in 2010. It is the way a number of Republicans would like insurance companies to operate again because covering pre-existing conditions cuts into the insurance companies' profits. Instead of saying judgment-laden comments like "Republicans are evil," it is more accurate to say that when it comes to public policy, Republicans often take positions that seem to reflect a lack of empathy. How else do you explain opposing medical coverage for those with pre-existing conditions, or Ronald Reagan being hesitant to support measures to combat poverty? It's not only Republicans. Many others, regardless of their political affiliations, may have a full measure of empathy when it comes to someone in their family, someone they know, or someone on "their team" (e.g. their school, people of their social class, people in their political party, etc.). But when it comes to someone who is not part of one's personal reference group, empathy can be muted or missing.

There are two main reasons why empathy needs to be central to our political process. First, we will all be better off for it. The more people who care about the hardships that all of us encounter from time to time, the more effectively we will address the issues of suffering within our society. Second, millions of potential voters in our society are turned off by the insensitivity of our political process and many of the people who run it. These disaffected citizens, many of whom fall under the umbrella of political introverts, regularly choose to not get involved in politics.

We generally think that the reason why people don't vote is because of apathy. Yes, that's an important factor, but for many people the political process is so distasteful that they just want to stay away from it. If there would be ways to get non-voting empathetic people to participate, these individuals could provide much of the necessary care and compassion to improve the way in which we do politics. \

By their very nature, political introverts tend to fly under the radar. We should not confuse this with thinking that they want to be invisible. They want their views to be part of our political dialogue. Their ideas are strong and often quiet. It behooves all candidates, introverts, extroverts, or ambiverts, to dial in to what political introverts are quietly thinking and saying.

In our focus group drawn from introverted, educated non-voters, there was a consensus that current politics do not provide realistic ways to express compassion. The group went on to provide helpful information on how to make voting a more welcoming experience for those who are either empathetic or introverted, or both, and who currently choose not to exercise their right and freedom to vote.

Throughout America's history, we have had statespersons who have expressed empathy in an authentic and articulate fashion. Here is an example from Robert Kennedy on the evening of

Dr. Martin Luther King's assassination, April 4, 1968. Senator Kennedy addressed a crowd of low-income African-Americans in Indianapolis, IN. He said:

"What we need in the United States is not division; what we need in the United States is not hatred; what we need in the United States is not violence and lawlessness, but is love, and wisdom, and compassion toward one another, and a feeling of justice toward those who still suffer within our country, whether they be white or whether they be black.[4]"

While over one hundred American cities had riots in the wake of Dr. King's assassination, Indianapolis did not. Many think the way in which Robert Kennedy could relate to the distraught and angry crowd is why Indianapolis stayed calm.

You can take Kennedy's remarkable words, spoken in a very high-tension situation when violence could easily have broken out, and extrapolate them to a universal strategy for how we should collectively regard one another. His empathy is a basis for forming public policy. He modeled a way of responding to tragedy by pulling a society together, rather than apart, when tensions are high.

Two months later, Robert Kennedy was assassinated in Los Angeles after winning the California Democratic Primary and in all likelihood the Democratic nomination for president in 1968. The last surviving Kennedy son, Teddy, eulogized his brother and said:

"My brother need not be idealized, or enlarged in death beyond what he was in life; to be remembered simply as a good and decent man, who saw wrong and tried to right it, saw suffering and tried to

---

4   https://en.wikisource.org/wiki/Speech_on_the_Assassination_of_
Martin_Luther_King,_Jr.

heal it, saw war and tried to stop it.[5]"

Ted Kennedy had just lost the third of three older brothers, all of whom had fallen to violence, two by means of assassination. His personal loss was extreme. Yet, instead of embellishing the life of his just fallen brother, Teddy placed Bobby on a level to which everyone could both relate and aspire. His words focused on the common good, something that can only be seen through the lens of empathy.

It would be reckless to paint all of today's politicians with a broad brush and say they don't provide America with what it needs. Barack Obama was a remarkable leader, who unfortunately was hamstrung by extreme ideologues who opposed virtually everything that he proposed. The contrast between him and his successor, Donald Trump, serves to shine a light on the integrity that Obama brought to the White House. Obama had the sharp mind of the law school professor that he was, but he seemed to lack the political savvy to successfully duel with the likes of Senate Majority Leader Mitch McConnell. Obama's empathy was nowhere more evident than the pain he felt every time another mass shooting occurred. His concern for the victims and their families was only matched by his frustration with the N.R.A. and other gun proponents.

As we write, Pete Buttigieg may well be developing into the type of leader we need. He is the first openly gay candidate to seek the nomination of a major party. Among his strengths is his ability to relate to those who have been oppressed and who need a new voice in Washington.

Elizabeth Warren is a visionary who doubles as a policy wonk.

---

5   https://www.americanrhetoric.com/speeches/ekennedytributetorfk.html

Her work to lobby for the creation of the Consumer Protection Agency reflects her commitment to protecting those who are economically abused by roughshod financial institutions. And Bernie Sanders should never be forgotten. He has the authenticity of personality and convictions that set him apart from most others in the field.

Whether solutions to our problems come from Democrats, Republicans, or a third party, our political process and the quality of life in the United States will not significantly improve until we find ways to increase the amount of empathy within us and amongst us.

How do we find and attract better political candidates and simultaneously more informed voters who can truly recognize a sensitive or empathetic candidate when they see one?

The answer may be surprising. The greatest impediment to making our society more caring and responsive is the nature of our schools. You might think that schools have nothing to do with politics, however, along with parents, they are the preeminent force that shape the kind of people our youth become when they reach adulthood.

The problem is not so much that our schools do not do a good job of teaching empathy. The problem goes beyond that. If you asked most educators how to teach empathy, they would run to their graduate studies and then put together a curriculum to teach empathy.

This in a nutshell is why our schools are not helping us become a more empathetic and compassionate society. The answer to teaching empathy has nothing to do with a curriculum. It has everything to do with teachers treating students with empathy. The teachers have to model empathy so that students know what it is. The next step is for the students to emulate it, something they can rarely do unless they have actually seen it and experienced its direct impact upon them.

This becomes a chicken and egg conundrum. How do you get teachers to model empathy for students if the teachers themselves have not been treated that way?

Here's a quick suggestion. Eliminate schools of education and let potential teachers develop their skills in a more natural fashion. Teaching is unlike any other profession. Graduating high school students have spent approximately ten thousand hours in classrooms. Graduates have seen good teachers, bad teachers, and virtually every variety in between. Ask any graduating senior what makes a good teacher and they can immediately tell you. Answers will include "they care about you," "they're fair," "they know their subject matter," "they have a good sense of humor," and "they are not afraid to show their own vulnerabilities." Not one of these things are naturally learned when pursuing a degree in education. The field of education studies exists because self-appointed educators created it. They convinced university administrators that it could be another profit-making field of study, and then linked their existence to state boards of education that control teacher certification.

It's going to take at least a generation to undo this mess. Teaching is not rocket science, like for instance, rocket science. Most of us know upon high school graduation what it takes to become a good teacher. Not everyone would be qualified, because inevitably some would be lacking in empathy, knowledge of subject, fairness, humor, and communication skills.

But for the few who have the personality traits to become good teachers, we need to provide ways for them to flourish. They need to learn more about the subject matter they will teach. But most importantly, their post high school experiences must be ones in which they further enhance their self-esteem, learn more about respecting others, develop a fuller understanding of societal problems, and enhance their understanding of how teaching is not just the transference of facts. Most importantly it is modeling healthy human relations and thoughtfully sharing that with their students. Finally, teaching is central to developing an informed and empathetic citizenry. If we teach with empathy, our political process will become much more caring about those in need. A progressive political agenda will never succeed without first developing more empathy among its individual citizens.

Chapter 2
THE NEED FOR CRITICAL THINKING

C RITICAL THINKING AND empathy are intricately linked. When they are in harmony, we get public policy that is responsive to the needs of people, particularly those who are suffering. When critical thinking and empathy are not in harmony, then we get harsh and insensitive policies.

A good definition of critical thinking is the logical analysis of facts to form a judgment. To give the definition a little more meat, it's helpful to add that it includes the rational, skeptical, unbiased analysis, evaluation, of factual evidence.

In a Venn Diagram, empathy and critical thinking overlap, and the common ground represents compassionate, thoughtful decisions.

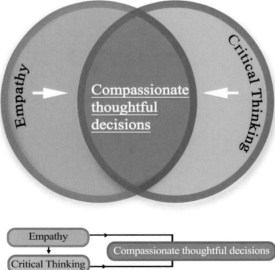

Empathy requires putting oneself in someone else's shoes. This means that we must have insight to know where the other person's shoes are and how that person got there. Figuring this out involves critical thinking, specifically the ability to evaluate facts in a rational, skeptical, unbiased way. We could not have empathy without the ability to think critically.

Similarly, critical thinking, at least when we are considering human behavior, requires empathy. Creating logical solutions to problems humans face requires the ability to consider the interests of all the relevant parties to a dispute or issue. For instance, an empathetic city planner researching the feasibility and desirability of creating a new eight-lane interstate highway that would run through a residential neighborhood would look at the highway's traffic benefits and, simultaneously, factor in how many people in the neighborhood would be displaced by the highway, where those residents would be able to find nearby affordable housing and the impact on nearby schools, businesses and social service agencies. She would concurrently factor in how many people in the neighborhood would be displaced by the highway, where those current residents would be able to find nearby affordable housing and what would happen to nearby schools, businesses and social service agencies.

The process would be complicated, and if there would be a workable solution, it would require thinking in a logical fashion while having compassion towards those who might get the short end of the stick. One of our nation's greatest assets are government officials (often known as bureaucrats) who can wisely assess data and make recommendations that are rational and responsive to the needs of the people.

Like empathy, critical thinking seems to be in short supply among many of our political leaders and also large segments of our body politic. Sloppy thinking is what makes us susceptible to fake news. I'm not talking about the "fake news" that Donald Trump alleges comes from the New York Times or the Washington Post; I'm talking about the kind of fake news illustrated in the narrative below.

Here's a case where the ability to think critically is essential to decipher the truth. You may recall a story called "Pizzagate" from the 2016 presidential election between Hillary Clinton and Donald Trump. The story emanated from email stolen by WikiLeaks from Clinton's campaign manager, John Podesta. In an effort to demean and demonize Clinton's character, the fable falsely claimed that the emails contained coded messages referring to human trafficking and connected several U.S. restaurants and high-ranking officials of the Democratic Party with an alleged child sex ring involving the restaurant and pizzeria Comet Ping Pong, located on Connecticut Avenue, NW in Washington, D.C.

The story was patently false, but the conspiracy theory went viral during the presidential election cycle. While the account has been extensively discredited and debunked by the Metropolitan Police Department of the District of Columbia, members of the alt-right and other opponents of Clinton's presidential campaign spread the conspiracy theory on social media outlets such as 4chan and Twitter. A man from North Carolina traveled to Comet Ping Pong to investigate this conspiracy, during which time he fired a rifle inside the restaurant. In addition, the restaurant owner and staff received death threats.

It is bad enough that conspirators on the far right bought into the story and even resorted to violence aimed at a thoroughly innocent target. But what is disturbing is how many people who for one reason or another hated Hillary Clinton were willing to place credence in the Pizzagate story, no matter how absurd it was.

In our current political climate, when we have operatives who have few scruples, as well as the capacity to access dozens of modes of social media. They can infect the body politic with misinformation at speeds that were never previously possible. Inaccurate news spreads quickly, virally. The shenanigans of these manipulators would not be such a problem if the body politic could see falsehood and immediately tamp down the flames of lies, but many voters are gullible, or simply not aware of the deviousness of political operatives. Thus, the ground is fertile for the spread of fake news.

Fake news does not always go viral, but one myth at a time, it can distort the thinking of otherwise believing citizens and further undermine the confidence of already skeptical voters. An example of incredulous political thinking came to me when I was interviewing a shopkeeper in suburban St. Louis on his why he was skeptical of politicians. He recounted a story of a woman who was a regular client at his store:

"I remember when Obama got elected, there was a lady who came into the store. She said, "Mr. Obama was here, and he gave me a lot of money. He told me to get this to the people."

The shopkeeper asked, "How much money did he give you?"

The woman said, "He gave me a blank check. And I'm going to

get this to the people."

The vendor said, "Next time I saw her, she was driving a new Cadillac. She had on a new full-length fur coat. I don't know who this lady was, but the next time I saw her, she drove a different Cadillac. Wore a different fur coat. And at that point, I didn't even want to know more. I didn't want to say anything."

In the interest of fairness, I suppose there is a one-tenth of one percent chance everything the shopkeeper describes is one hundred percent accurate, including this woman receiving a direct payment from Barack Obama. But I'm betting against it. One reason is that there is not a trace of evidence that Barack Obama, or anyone in his campaigns, ever did anything like this—anytime, anyplace, under any circumstances. If a story is going to be true, it would help to have corroborating evidence. The vendor simply did not have it, likely no fault of his own. He only sporadically watched the news, and his news outlet of choice was Fox. Somewhere along the line, he did not develop the necessary critical thinking skills to detect truth from fiction in the world of politics. Are people to blame if they grow from childhood to adulthood not acquiring the necessary thinking skills to question the journalistic integrity of certain media outlets?

On a larger scale, as late as 2017, over fifty percent of Republicans believed that Barack Obama was born in Kenya[6]. When people are gullible to this kind of misinformation, meaningful, productive exchanges of political ideas are nearly impossible. This lack of accurate information ultimately impacts the decisions that leaders

---

6   https://www.newsweek.com/trump-birther-obama-poll-republicans-kenya-744195

make to guide the country. Somehow our schools are failing to provide many students with the basics of b.s. detection.

Why is it that as a society, the United States has more difficulty than other industrialized countries in establishing governmental norms that includes a safety net for citizens that provides necessary assistance for people who are young, ill, infirmed, old, or economically poor? Every other industrialized nation in the world has a health care system that one way or another guarantees access to care for all citizens, and at affordable prices.

It might be helpful to draw upon our history and look back at the establishment of our country. The northern territories were largely colonized by a particular group of white Europeans who were among the first to emigrate to this country. These Puritans brought with them an ethic that played a formative role in characterizing the early years of America.

What essentially is the Puritan ethic? Historically, it has been a work ethic in which theology and standard values emphasize hard work, discipline, and frugality. To many, success in life is a result of a person's subscription to the values espoused by the Protestant faith, particularly Calvinism.

The Puritan ethic subscribes to the notion that those who prosper economically do so because they are "chosen," or that they are God's people who are being rewarded for their faith. Conversely, those who live in poverty are often responsible for their own misfortune, regardless of the circumstances that may have led to them to hard times.

In the early years of settlement and development, the thought leaders in what was to become the United States were not thinking empathetically about the economic well-being of everyone. Rather they subscribed to scriptural teaching that some people were simply better than others. In modern America, we would call this a "values agenda" rather than an economic agenda designed to benefit all.

Nowhere is this clearer than in Thomas Frank's 2007 book, *What's the Matter with Kansas*. Frank describes Kansas as a state that in recent years has chosen to embrace certain "values issues" such as being anti-abortion rights or anti-gay. Concurrently, Kansas has not addressed the declining economic plight of many farmers and former blue-collar workers who have lost their jobs and the unions that protected them.[7] As "values" have become more important in Kansas, economic opportunities have been reduced. When citizens' economic concerns are forgotten and when some are punished for how they make personal decisions on issues like abortion, the society becomes more and more devoid of empathy.

This phenomenon is not unique to Kansas. Look at West Virginia. This is a state that used to be true blue. It was created in 1861 when it seceded from Virginia due to Virginia's Confederate affiliations. Historically it supported Democrats because the New Deal supported its miners and other economically challenged citizens. But Republicans were able to fashion a line of thinking that went counter to decades of convictions of coal-miners, both in and out of work. For all these many years, coal miners had accurately seen the coal companies as their oppressors. The companies paid workers poorly and the corporations frequently did not implement or follow government safety standards for the mines. They

---

7   In the Blue Wave of 2018, Kanas elected a Democratic Governor, Laura Kelly, and Democratic Rep. Sharice Davids to the U.S. House. She is an openly gay Native American.

essentially treated the miners as share-croppers because when the miners were not at work, they could only rent their homes or buy their goods and services, including food, from company-owned stores. It may be summed up best in the 1946 song, "Sixteen Tons," written by Merle Travis and famously sung in 1955 by Tennessee Ernie Ford with the clinching line, "I owe my soul to the company store."

Over the past fifty years in West Virginia and elsewhere in Appalachia, Republicans have successfully convinced miners that their company employers truly cared about them. Their reasoning was that workers only did well when the company prospered. That was only half-true. Sometimes the workers did well when the companies profited; other times the companies profited in part by squeezing every last dime out of the laborers.

Republicans convinced many workers that the ogre was the government because it did not always support coal as the country's primary energy source. Under certain administrations, government policies reflected concern about the inefficiency of coal and other fossil fuels, and the reality that they created enormous environmental damage. To make things worse, Republicans have, and continue to, resist bringing new alternate energy industries into the former areas where coal was king.

The Republican mantra that "government is the enemy" spread from the hollers of Appalachia to the rusted factories of the upper Midwest, and ultimately, across the entire country. It was government regulations that kept American automobiles from being affordable and desirable. It was the government that promoted international trade which hurt American producers.

What Republicans did not tell these workers whose jobs began to and eventually disappeared was that when they shopped at Wal-Mart, virtually all of their low-cost goods came from overseas. Those living in or near poverty could not have it both ways; tariffs to protect their aging industries and inexpensive merchandise from the likes of Wal-Mart that is manufactured in China and other low-wage countries.

But perhaps the most important factor that drove those in poverty away from the Democratic Party was how they saw the new members of the Democratic Party. We're talking about those who hold white-collar professional jobs. Frank describes them most acerbically in his 2016 book, *Listen Liberal.*

These modern Democratic professionals do not have dirt under their fingernails and grime around their collars as their Democratic parents and grandparents had. The Democratic professional class have shiny shoes on their feet and the walls in their offices and homes that are plastered with diplomas, awards, and other acknowledgements of some sort of merit.

The ways in which professionals view themselves is similar to how other groups that make up the fabric of America identify themselves. As liberals, they have empathy, but most of it is for themselves and people who are like them. Similar to every other group, they want to protect their own interests. There are liberal intellectuals who predicted that the new class of professionals would extend empathy out to the traditional Democratic base of old. Yes, liberals talk about caring for those in racial minorities, mostly children. But if advancing the causes of those who suffer means sacrifice on their own part, then personal economic sacrifice becomes problematic. This compassion would inevitably involve higher taxes. While these professionals who have progressive political views may be more supportive than conservatives to the notion that government services must be paid for, they are still reluctant to see their own taxes go up, even if the reason is to tighten our safety net and help the most distressed among us.

When the professionals engage in critical thinking about public policy, the empathy that they feel is often directed towards protecting their own interests. Who can blame them? Every other group does so.

Today's progressives are likely to support a new cultural center in their community but at the same time oppose constructing a homeless shelter close to where they live. Redistributing wealth, a one-time staple of the Democratic Party, has become less of a priority for many professionals who identify themselves as Democrats.

Why does the arc of critical thinking skills and empathy of professional Americans decreasingly extend to the less fortunate? Part of it may be the Puritan ethic, but religious tenets do not tell the whole story. We must also direct our focus on our educational system because our schools largely turn a blind eye to the public good. School administrators, like other professionals, are mainly concerned with protecting themselves and their interests. Promoting the common good is rarely a high priority for them.

A good first question about schools is why they exist in their current form. We are led to believe that their primary function is to educate children: to create and ensure a better society. But here's where a little cynicism and a lot of reality is needed. Schools exist for the same reason as every other institution in society—to "stay in business," to protect themselves, to self-perpetuate. Whatever keeps them in good stead with their constituencies (parents, students, teachers, government officials, and perhaps most importantly, professional educators higher up the bureaucratic chain) dictates the path to be followed. As we will see in the next chapter, breaking up the entrenched forces in our schools and their administrative bureaucracies is the first step we must take to allow empathy and critical thinking to become the main characteristics of our schools and ultimately our society at large.

Our schools are currently obsessed with statistical analysis of how they do. Measuring the growth of our children needs far more humane methods of assessment than numbers. Straight statistical analysis is better reserved for sports like baseball than the development of children. In baseball, a batting average tells us what percentage of the time a batter gets a hit. An earned run average tells us in nine-inning increments how effective a pitcher has been in containing opposing hitters. In recent years, we have entered an era of sabermetrics in which analysts drill down further and further to analyze how well a hitter or pitcher is doing. We now know what percentage of the time a batter hits a ground ball that goes through the infield for a hit. We know how many times a pitcher's curveball rotates from the time it leaves his hand until it crosses the plate. All of this gives baseball aficionados literally millions of points of data from which to make analyses of how well a player is performing. It also provides a platform for projections as to how well a player can be expected to perform in the future.

But there are limitations to how much the numbers can tell

us. Baseball is like life: it literally throws us lots of curveballs. We can't anticipate the unexpected. Will a player get injured, will he have marital problems that impact his game, will he have a crisis of confidence, get the yips?

There are also the intangibles like how much a player contributes by being a positive influence in the clubhouse. Or is he like a cancer on the team, stirring up trouble with other players? These are factors that simply cannot be measured.

If you want to know how a baseball player is doing right now, the conclusions we can draw from a statistical analysis are remarkably valuable.

Baseball, however, is not public policy. Measuring the effectiveness of governmental programs is much more difficult than evaluating a baseball player.

For example, the current level of poverty in the United States is $25,750 for a family of four. We can measure what percentage of the population is above or below that number at any given point in time, but each family has its own story. Some are saddled with deep medical expenses. Others have members who have near-term prospects for a well-paying job. Others can't scrape together the necessary money for a high school graduate to go to college. The poverty line is helpful, but sound policy about addressing the problems of the poor has to be much more comprehensive than relying on one number.

We spend hundreds of billions each year on the military. What is our ROI (return on investment)? If in a given year the United States avoids armed conflict with another country, does that make all of our military spending worthwhile? Or should we consider the opportunity costs for spending that money on the military?

What impact would that money have on addressing homelessness, working on cures for cancer and other diseases, or modernizing our infrastructure? These are all difficult questions, and while statistical analysis is important, it can be useless if our leaders cannot address these questions with empathy towards all citizens involved, combined with critical thinking that helps us prioritize what the country needs.

The growth of social sciences over the past century has led to an effort to measure just about anything. We often lose sight of what value, if any, there is to measuring. Nowhere is this more evident than in the field of education. The United States has developed a huge industry in test-taking for educational institutions. The profession of educational bureaucrats (edu-crats) is based on the validity of testing and the scores that we accumulate from the testing.

In the sixties and seventies, some efforts were made to humanize education, to focus more on the needs of the "whole child" including his or her emotional well-being, physical health, pleasure while in school. We had a growing number of teachers who were inclined to work with students in a holistic way; one that addressed each student's individual needs and fashioned strategies to maximize that student's personal growth. But this movement was smothered by the testing monolith that stood to gain billions of dollars by essentially forcing schools to buy into the concept that administering tests, grading them, and making life-changing decisions based on the results was what was needed.

As we will further examine in the next chapter, the testing

industry is one of the biggest reasons why our schools do little to teach critical thinking and to encourage empathy among teachers and students alike.

Similarly, our political leaders will continue to take advantage of an unsuspecting electorate unless both the politicians and the public come to place more value on the common good. The common good remains an afterthought to many because it requires empathy to truly think beyond one's own personal needs and desires. Welcoming political introverts into the process can go a long way toward humanizing politics and rending decisions with better critical thinking and more empathy.

Chapter 3

MAKING OUR SCHOOLS MORE EMPATHETIC

I NSTEAD OF BEGINNING this chapter with stories about how our educational system is doing a disservice to our children, let's begin with how the system is doing a disservice to American adults.

In 2016, Donald Trump was almost legitimately elected president of the United States; he came within nearly three million votes in the popular vote. Through the antiquated and undemocratic Electoral College, he became president by default. How could the American people be party to that? Almost all of the sixty-three million individuals who voted for him are products of the American education system and that may tell us something about how he could become president.

Ninety percent of American adults have earned high school degrees, meaning they have spent at least ten thousand hours in classrooms. Yet, most high school graduates have difficulty naming the three branches of our government. Only eight percent of U.S. high school seniors could identify slavery as the central cause of the Civil War. Forty percent do not know that Congress has the power to declare war. Many students do not know the difference between a country and a city.

It is fair to ask what portion of those ten thousand hours in school were productive. How much time was spent staring out the window, memorizing facts for a test that were forgotten the following day, taking courses that were of little or no interest to those in the class?

If we only focus on the cognitive information that high school graduates do not learn, then we miss the primary area in which our educational system is failing. Students are not learning about protecting and advancing the common good in America. In fact, many know very little about the concept of the common good. Schools often tend to give students a myopic view of the world which does not include much beyond the particular world in which they live.

Big happenings in schools are homecoming week, sporting events, prom, and the occasional school play. Considerable time is spent bragging about classes that students are taking or complaining about teachers or assignments. Gossip is often the coin of the realm. The world of school is big enough to make it seem like the entire universe. School personnel prefer students to be thoroughly into the world of school. It makes what they, the administrators, teachers, and other staff, do seem more important.

What about all the other people who inhabit the students' communities, their country, their planet? How can students care about what their country is really like or how to make the world more peaceful and ecologically healthy if their primary view of community is almost exclusively their school? How can we as a country find political leaders who promote the wellness of our entire community if many Americans are locked into their own worlds which are much smaller than our national or international communities? The result is that we recently selected for president someone who is more of an entertainer, and a bad one at that, than a philosopher and pragmatist of governance.

To truly care about the common good, one must be capable of feeling empathy in a way that reaches beyond one's own personal world. That is not happening in America to the degree necessary for a compassionate and understanding world. Some schools or school districts may have mission statements that reference empathy, but the way in which they structure learning tends to undermine what students need most to become more empathetic—teachers who model it in the classroom. Where is the empathy in tests and long assignments?

We as citizens must learn how to act empathetically in the political world to promote the adoption of policies that are compassionate and well-reasoned. One step that we can take is for those who have a vision for improving our society, but who choose not to vote, to become engaged and help us find candidates who are worthy of earning their votes. If schools can better awaken students to the dramatic needs of our national and global communities, then we will have more active voters and hopefully better leaders.

To better understand the low priority that empathy has in most classrooms, let's go back to basics about schools. Why do schools exist? They exist for the same reason as every other institution in our world: to self-perpetuate. The worst thing that could happen to a school is not if students are below grade level on arbitrary standardized tests, or if the football team has a forty-three-game losing streak or if there is racial discord within its walls. The worst thing that could happen is for the school to close. That could happen in any number of ways, none of which are good. In the case of a private school, demand for admission could decline to the point that the school is no longer financially viable. In the case of a public school, the demand could also decline as students and parents use every technique available to move to another school or district. Generally, this happens to a school if it gets a bad reputation, and as we all know, reputation can be quite different from reality. But it doesn't matter, every school wants to be regarded highly. Image is key to survival, not the reality of what actually goes on within the walls of the school community.

During the years that I was director of an independent secondary school in St. Louis, dealing with the pressures of promoting image was the most vexing challenge I faced, along with the related issue of raising money. Parents did not spend the time in the building that students and teachers did, so the parents only "had a clue" as to what actually happened in school. While the top priority for many parents was the well-being of their child, for others it was for the school to have an image about which they could brag. When it came to asking parents and others for money (a terribly odious task which eventually drove me to another vocation), the product that we were largely selling was image, less so the complexities of trying to make a school work well for the students and teachers who live in the building each day. The best that I could do was to try to have all staff be "as real as possible" in the building so that we had maximum possible authenticity to the students. We tried as best as possible to shield students from our bullshit peddling of image enhancement.

If image is central to how we view our schools, could that relate to how image is so fundamental to the way in which political candidates market themselves? This question is not frequently asked, but by trying to answer it, we learn a great deal about how our political system is so shallow. Why is whether a candidate marches in the Labor Day parade more important than if she has a strong platform on worker safety? Why is it that what she wears in the parade is more closely scrutinized than the vested interests from whom she gets the bulk of her campaign money?

There are several ways in which schools try to build their image. One is by what can be measured, such as standardized test scores. Whether test scores tell us anything about what students are really learning is a question that is not asked. What is important is that tests can be scored. Thus, when the test scores are up, these numbers can be touted when the school promotes itself. There is often a lack of honesty to this reporting; we know that there are times when the test scores that are reported have been altered.

When a school is test-obsessed, students are living in silos with walls that are covered with questions that do not encourage students to think critically or with empathy. The game consists of students being asked largely meaningless questions and then choosing the correct circle to fill in with the number two pencil. But what if the student wants to jump out of the silo and learn about that whole world stretching outside these boundaries? For a student to explore the world beyond rote, he or she will need a special kind of teacher, one who gets excited when students have insights rather than just correct answers to narrowly focused questions.

I have repeatedly seen bright and sensitive students become discouraged because they did not test well, either on the standardized or classroom tests. When teachers tell students that they just have to work harder, the teachers are not expressing compassion, and this strategy rarely works. What is needed from teachers is awareness that students, like adults, have differing learning styles. Assessing how a student is doing cannot be measured by a single form of evaluation. If teachers want to encourage students to do better, they have to be sensitive to which pathway to success works best for each student.

What else do we measure in schools? Classroom grades as well as standardized tests. How are grades determined? Often from tests, tests that may or may not accurately reflect the material covered in class. How much of the information that students correctly give on tests do they remember the next day or the next week? That is a question that schools do not like to ask.

Essays are more subjective than objective tests, but what if the teacher does not like what a particular student has to say, or how he or she says it?

If there is no accurate way to measure student "achievement," should we stop trying? No. How students do in areas of evaluation can be important indicators of how much they are learning. The problem is placing so much importance on test scores and grades.

Schools have to be fun. Here's why. We all spend at least ten thousand hours in them when we are young, and wouldn't you rather have ten thousand of enjoyment rather than boredom? If a person lives to be ninety years old, he will have lived one-fifth of his life in school, and that's even before college. Think of the negative impact of most of those hours being boring and unpleasant.

If you don't believe that large numbers of students are bored at school, read the report from Live Science Magazine[8].

"School can be a real yawn. Two out of three high-school students in a large survey say they are bored in class every single day.

It might not seem startling to learn that kids don't like school or that they are bored *sans* computer games, text-message time and freedom to roam the Internet. But the underlying reasons for the boredom are significant and troubling, according to a report released today.

About 30 percent of the students indicate they are bored due to lack of interaction with teachers and 75 percent report material being taught is not interesting."

If you're largely bored in school, what are you thinking about? For some, this time can be very productive. In the sciences, great examples are Albert Einstein, Steve Jobs, and Bill Gates. Many artists created their greatest works, or at least the origins of their greatest works, while they were doodling in school. But for far too many students, the time spent while bored in school is filled with banal thoughts such as how many times does the minute hand of the clock have to rotate before I can get out of here. They might be having deep thoughts about the nose of the teacher, or if there is anything edible for lunch. Then there is another group of people who are having thoughts of meanness, who they might bully or why they really can't stand so-and-so. We have become all too familiar with what can happen to students who feel alienated and deeply depressed while in school.

I learned a great deal about how to try to teach from observing

---

8   https://en.wikipedia.org/wiki/Calvinism

my own K12 teachers over those first ten thousand hours. I learned different lessons in the summers from the more than one thousand hours I spent with camp counselors. The counselors were individuals who had a primary mandate of making life fun, and I was fortunate enough to have many who were very skilled at this mandate. Why were they good at it? I would say primarily because they were fun people; they had not had the *joie de vivre* squeezed out of them. Most were naturals; there was no need for them to be trained for months, or even years to become a camp counselor.

I was director of a school for fifteen years. Hiring new teachers was never easy. In retrospect, we made some terrific decisions and we also made mistakes. But one thing that helped me was that I always looked for individuals who had been camp counselors. That's usually where our conversations could begin. Why? Because that's where you can tell if a teaching candidate is really interested in the holistic development of a child. If the applicant only wants to talk about which books he would like students to read or how far they should get in eighth grade Algebra, then I was talking to someone whose main agenda was quite different from the overall healthy development of the student.

This brings up an important question about teacher-to-student ratios in the classroom. My first year of teaching was fifth grade in the St. Louis Public Schools. At that time (1969), if a male of draft age taught in an inner-city school, he would get a deferment from the draft. For any number of reasons, I did not want to go to Vietnam, so I felt very fortunate to get the teaching job.

I learned of my teaching assignment a couple of days before school began. I was assigned to Dozier School (long since torn down) in north St. Louis. I had forty students in the class.

Whatever skills I brought from my years as a camp counselor were of little benefit in this teaching situation. The student-to-teacher ratio was forty to one. Some of the students were genuinely interested in learning, others were just marking time, even at the age of eleven or twelve. For many of the students in this one hundred percent African-American classroom, there was the novelty of having a white teacher. This was an era when there were ongoing rebellious feelings and occasional acts by African-Americans towards whites. I felt much of the anger within the students and thought it was well-deserved. But my understanding/empathy did nothing to help me maintain control of the class.

One day the African-American Curriculum Coordinator for the school came into the classroom and the kids immediately came to order. What did she do? She told them to "straighten up or else." Then in front of the class, she told me that if I wanted to gain control, I had to do the same thing, tell them to straighten up or else. I think that she was overlooking a primary difference between her and me. I could mouth the words, but I did not have the mean stare that she could flash at the students.

After ten weeks on the north side, I was transferred to the south side, to an all-white school named after the educator Horace Mann. Again, forty students and fifth grade. I don't know if I wanted things to get better or not. Yes, I wanted my days to be less miserable, but at the same time I did not want to think that these white students were inherently more cooperative than African-American students whom I had taught five miles to the north.

I found the answer to my question before lunch on the first day.

There were some great kids, but the critical mass was out of control. There were times when the principal, a slender, stoic white man named Glenn Campbell, would come into the classroom, pace the aisles and stare at the students. The kids immediately shaped up. He never had to say a word.

But my experiences with the students at both schools were hardly all bad. On weekends, my fiancé, who was also teaching in the St. Louis Public Schools, and I would take as many of our students as we could pack into our car on field trips. We may have had four or five kids at a time. Whether it was the art museum or a ballgame or just playing in a park, it was without exception enjoyable and hopefully a learning experience for the kids, as well as for us. It almost seemed like redemption for all the miserable Monday through Friday times when both we and the students suffered. The weeks were made enjoyable by having these enriching and enjoyable experiences on the weekends.

A lot of why I did not fare well in the fifth-grade classrooms had to do with my inability to give that mean stare. But a lot also had to do with forty students in the classroom.

The next year I was fortunate enough to land a job teaching high school at a private suburban school. Each class had about fifteen students and I was teaching areas that I truly loved such as American History and Contemporary Affairs. At that time, there were virtually no Advanced Placement (AP) classes to increase the workload on students, their bragging, and their moaning and groaning. During that year, I found my voice in teaching. In the classes, we spent a lot of time on the subject matter, but we also did a lot of BS-ing in class. I think that it was relaxing and engaging for everyone.

I took a somewhat different approach to teaching American History, having a certain irreverence about our heroes and other leaders. However, the assassinations of President John F. Kennedy, Dr. Martin Luther King and Senator Robert Kennedy were still fresh in our minds. These men were role models from whom we could learn so much, not only about public policy, but also about "how to be."

In some ways the political situation in the late sixties and early seventies was not too different from today. How could a nation see three such outstanding individuals slain in cold blood and then elect as our leader Richard Nixon? Memory lapses of this magnitude are one of the reasons why I believe we continue to do so many things fundamentally wrong in this country in both education and politics. The problems are generational and somehow, we have to break the non-productive cycles we are in. How could we force Richard Nixon out of office in 1974 and forty-two years later select the likes of Donald Trump without expecting Trump to provide more of the same, and worse? In spite of all our new standardized tests, AP classes, and fancy college brochures, we really have not advanced a bit when it comes to choosing leaders who can help us move our society forward in positive directions. No nation with empathetic voters who think critically should ever come close to putting a Richard Nixon or Donald Trump in the White House.

I have had a lot of short-comings as a teacher. My preparation has not always been up to the task. My ability to find the best resources for individual students was lacking at times. I don't know if this counts or not, but I had (and still have) a potty mouth.

Despite that, I do think that I was decent at modeling empathy. What I offered was nothing that had been specifically taught to me by anyone; rather it came from observing and learning from other people in positions of power, some of whom had abused their positions and others who had been incredibly sensitive to those with whom they were working.

Whatever empathy I had was consistent with my political views. I have always felt pain for those among us who suffer. In all societies, those who suffer generally fall into two categories—those whose human rights are being abused and those who are economically deprived.

These two groups are often like a Venn Diagram with a tremendous amount of overlap. If our political process does not address the needs of those within the diagram, then we remain as imperfect as we ever have been. No matter how many American flags adorn the porches of homes in small towns or how many times "God Bless America" is sung during the seventh inning stretch, we are not moving ahead. We have to sing a different tune, and that begins with how teachers treat students in classrooms. The more high school graduates we have who are low on the empathy scale, the more likely we will be to continue to elect the likes of Nixon and Trump as inequity within the society increases.

Finding a way to bring more teachers into classrooms who are empathetic is only a start. It will take decades or even generations for the supply of empathetic teachers to grow. Rather than looking for the kind of quick fixes to problems that define the current strategies of both schools and politics, we need to begin long journeys towards collaboratively improving our schools and our political system.

Problems with schools can also be found by following the money. This leads us into the twin worlds of universities and school bureaucracies. There are currently close to four hundred graduate schools of education in the United States[9]. Over fifteen hundred colleges and universities offer undergraduate degrees in education, and this is not by accident[10]. After World War II, as more and more students went to college and our elementary and secondary schools were expanding as a result of the post-war baby boom, the need for teachers increased. Prior to that time, most college graduates who had received a major could apply to become a teacher. Generally, what they brought to the table was a fair amount of knowledge in one or two subject areas and a passion to work with children.

These teachers did not pursue the career for the money. In 1950, the average salary for a full-time teacher was $3,300. That would be slightly under $35,000 in 2019 dollars or just forty percent above the poverty level for a family of four[11]. Clearly, teaching was either a labor of love for many, or a disproportionate number of teachers were either single or not the primary wage-earners in their households.

In 1950, teaching was not an easy job and it still isn't easy now. Most other professions have advancement ladders that employees can climb to take on more responsibility and earn more money. This was true in education as well, but not to the same extent as in the fields of business or government administration.

---

9   https://www.usnews.com/best-graduate-schools/top-education-schools/edu-rankings

10   https://www.niche.com/colleges/search/best-colleges-for-education/?page=1

11   https://www.aier.org/cost-living-calculator; https://aspe.hhs.gov/poverty-guidelines

Teachers could rise to the levels of department chairs and principals of their schools. They rarely moved "upstairs" into the offices of the district superintendents. As public-school districts became larger, there was a growing need for more centralized administration. These district positions largely involved building management, finances and personnel. There were rarely whole sections devoted to curriculum. I remember my first year of teaching in 1969. On the day before school began, I was given several books and told, "Teach them." There had to be a better way than that, but what was needed was not the establishment of a bloated industry of curriculum experts.

Over the past fifty years, school administrations have ballooned. District offices are full of curriculum specialists, individuals who make a good living but whose jobs involve an inordinate amount of time interfering with the lives of classroom teachers. Because these positions of curriculum specialists now exist, teachers have much less room to be independent, self-resourceful and autonomous. They've become more like automatons. What is sacrificed is much of the empathy that naturally evolves as an autonomous teacher relates to his or her students.

The more that teachers are programmed, the less critical thinking is required of them, or is even permitted from them. The more teachers follow a script that is driven by a distant curriculum, the less focus they have on the well-being of the individual students. Whatever capacity a teacher had to feel empathy, and model empathy, was diminished by the encumbering restraints of the "on-demand" curricula forced upon them.

In my present job, which involves providing unique programs

focused on active citizenship for students, it is discouraging how many times we hear from teachers that they are not interested in enrichment programs for students because they don't want to fall a day behind in their curriculum.

In his farewell address as president in 1961, Dwight Eisenhower warned us of the power of the military-industrial complex. This took a great deal of courage from someone who spent most of his adult life in the military and depended on the products which that industry had provided to him and on those who served under his command.

Since 1961, many other bureaucracies have bloated. One of the biggest might be called the "university schools of education—state and local boards of education complex." For simplicity, let's just refer to it as the educracy. Through the decades, there has been a direct correlation between the growth of the educracy and the decline of empathy in the classrooms of our schools.

Many of us are familiar with the book *All I Really Need to Know I Learned in Kindergarten: Uncommon Thoughts on Common Things* by Robert Fulghum. The book contains a great deal of wisdom and insight. When it comes to empathy, we know that children as young as five understand when they are receiving compassion and understand when they are able to give it to others. For some of these five-year-olds, empathy stays with them throughout their lives. But in the modern world, sustaining empathy from childhood into adulthood has become a challenge. There are so many forces that work against our empathetic selves. Kids in first grade are being given homework and with each year, the pressure increases as do the consequences of not meeting the demands of teachers. It can become demoralizing and soon enough children see themselves in rat races. This pressure is a countervailing force to empathy.

We have to change the nature of our schools. We are up against highly entrenched economic and bureaucratic forces that have vested interests in keeping schools the way they are. And since these forces want schools to reflect that vague notion of "community standards," most people are quite happy with schools the way they are. Community standards are often set by the loudest voices, and since those voices are often conservative ones, schools are rarely agents of societal change.

What educrats give to schools is a gift that runs in reverse and never stops taking. In many public-school districts, if teachers want a pay increase (and most teachers are still terribly underpaid), then the path to augmenting income takes one right back into one of the tens of thousands of doors marked "Welcome to the House of Educrats." Colleges make millions upon millions of dollars from teachers who are essentially forced to take "continuing education" courses. Somehow our society has decided that it's acceptable for an overworked and stressed teacher to go to a college campus to take classes that are often mind-numbing, demeaning and demanding. Think of the opportunity costs. That teacher could instead be home having quality time with a child or could be just taking a walk in a park or reading a book for pleasure. But no, the educrats' monolith hangs on to teachers as long as it can. Teachers thought they were adults but learn they are not yet ready to be emancipated until the system squeezes the last dime or moment of free time from every teacher who is forced to play the game.

Since image is central to what schools want to promote, school administrators are kept busy dishing out mounds and mounds of bullshit to enhance people's perception of their institutions. If we are going to change this, we have to call on the resources of the best B.S. detectors in our society. Who are they? The children.

Spewing bullshit is in many ways learned behavior. It is not the way in which young children naturally talk with one another. Why does anyone spew bullshit? The primary reason is because dealing with the truth and honesty is more painful than covering it up.

If we are going to reduce the amount of bullshit in our schools, in our politics, and in society as a whole, we need to call on the resources of children who have not been terribly tainted by adulthood. I'm talking about taking on those characteristics of adults that are counterproductive to understanding what is really happening.

Year after year we have children in kindergarten who have a clearer moral fiber than many of the older students, as well as most of the adults in schools. As these children get older and move out of elementary school, their ability to decipher reality from B.S. diminishes. They need allies if they are going to maintain the ability to sense when B.S. is being shoveled their way.

This is why we need teachers who come from the relatively small number of adults who are good B.S. detectors. These individuals are likely ones who were able to go through school and keep their B.S. detectors sharp as they developed a keen sense of irony. Instead of consuming the B.S. in their schools, they were able to see it in perspective, laugh about it, and commit themselves to personally seeing through it and hopefully helping others do the same.

There is more than a kernel of truth in movies like *Ferris*

Bueller's Day Off or *Breakfast Club* in which schools are portrayed as often heartless and removed from the reality of the world in which students live. It takes special teachers to break out of the culture of B.S. that exists in most schools.

Who are these people who we need to become future teachers? They are people who can teach with a twinkle in their eye, who can make sure that the challenges are there for students, but who recognize that there is a certain absurdity about keeping kids caged up for x number of hours five days a week and then asking them to succumb to your demands at night for something called homework. These are people who can recognize the need for fun in school because all of us at all ages need fun in our lives.

These are also people who would be highly unlikely to spend years of their lives in education technique classes as undergraduates in college or to take graduate courses to get certified. Their focus in college would be to become more educated in fields of study that are of interest to them, which could well include education, but not at the exclusion of other areas. They would continue on the life-long journey of sharpening their critical thinking skills. Many could spend their summers as camp counselors, learning to "be real" with kids. What could be a better way to prepare to become a teacher?

All of this sounds very difficult, because it is. Whether we're talking about schools, our political process, or any other facet of our society, we need to maximize our resources in concentrated areas to make change. Empathy is the key to both a kinder and more productive society. We cannot artificially manufacture empathy. We cannot teach it through wonder curricula or weekend experiences. We need to make it a top priority in the way in which we model to children on a daily basis how to become adults.

The changes we need have begun in many places, mostly isolated from one another. But the path that we need to take is not an unknown one. Many have traveled it and become very generous empathetic citizens. In the early seventies in St. Louis, there were a half-dozen blossoming schools that were empathy oriented. Some prospered and still exist in a somewhat modified form; others were unable to secure the money to sustain themselves.

How can we get more teachers who model empathy into the classroom? It's like anything else in our economy, supply and demand. We need more young people who see the absurdity in much of school and want to help students become more caring empathetic citizens to make the choice to become teachers. Adequate pay will clearly help attract these people to become teachers as well as the fulfillment they find in working collaboratively and humanely with students and other empathetic teachers. At the same time, we need more and more schools to open up positions for these teachers who model empathy. That is the really tough part.

When it comes to public schools, either new teachers need to find ways to sneak through the bureaucratic and regulatory cracks, or look for opportunities in inner-city or rural districts where the districts have difficulty recruiting teachers and the districts will bend the rules in order to get them.

Private schools are not burdened by the same regulations as public schools. They are much more at liberty to hire the teachers they want. But building a model based on private schools is very difficult because private schools generally cater to families who can afford to pay tuition. That's a non-starter for major societal change.

SPECIAL WARNING: In the next several pages, we're going to use a word that is often offensive to liberals, and deservedly so. But please consider how experimenting with **vouchers** (yes, that word), if properly done, could provide ways to create new schools that could be based on empathy and critical thinking. No discrimination of any sort would be permitted. Here we go:

There is a way to make private schools part of the mainstream without costing families anything more than what they pay in taxes to public schools. It's called vouchers. Here's how it works. Rather than having the tax dollars that are allocated for each child to go to the public school district in which they live, the money instead becomes a voucher, or cash equivalency, which the family can use to pay tuition to the school of its choice. If a family likes the public school(s) that their children attend, then nothing has to change—the voucher would go to that public school directly from a family rather than going to a school board. If a family would prefer for a child to attend a private school which they previously could not afford, now they will have the ability to make that choice. They simply pay the private school with the school voucher that they and every other parent has for each of their children.

More importantly, when there are vouchers in the marketplace of schools, there are incentives for new schools to be established. New private schools could mirror public schools in some ways, but ideally with different ways of teaching, including a special emphasis on empathy. The schools could be designed to promote economic and social diversity. Some would concentrate more on the arts; others on STEM and others on making everything about school fun. Public schools would be free to also decentralize and innovate.

There are, however, clear down sides to vouchers. They have a long and ugly history of being used to create segregated academies, primarily in the South. There would have to be very strict regulations about non-discrimination. These regulations could be similar to those that were in the federal Voting Rights Act of 1965. Unfortunately, the John Roberts-led Supreme Court stripped away these regulations in *Shelby County v Holder* in 2013[12]. But then we need to ask whether we should allow religious schools to qualify for vouchers if you accept the premise of separation of church and state or if that particular religion teaches intolerance? What about schools that either through religion or some other means teach violence and disrespect? And perhaps most importantly, will the public be able to separate the substance of the schools that are part of the marketplace from the image that each of them tries to project? This is the real risk of a market-based system of schools—the b.s. that inevitably will surround it.

These questions are difficult and stand as impediments to creating workable voucher systems. But the biggest obstacle to vouchers is public schools themselves. It is not necessarily the schools, but the administrations that network them together. Vouchers are a tremendous threat to educrats, whether they live in school district offices or in government at the state or federal level. The reason is that most schools could exist independently from district or state boards. They could be lean and efficient. The opposition of educrats is in itself a pretty good indicator that vouchers are an idea that is definitely worth exploring.

---

12   https://en.wikipedia.org/wiki/Shelby_County_v._Holder

Vouchers were very much on my mind in 1974 when we started Crossroads. It was, and remains, an independent secondary school without religious affiliation. One of our reasons for starting the school was because we were quite upset with how racially segregated schools in St. Louis were (remember that just a few years previously I had taught in a fifth grade class that was one hundred percent African-American and then finished the year teaching a different fifth grade class that was one hundred percent Caucasian).

Four of the five initial teachers at Crossroads lived in a planned community in St. Louis which was racially balanced. We were able to secure space in a neighborhood community center to establish the school. We recruited fifty middle school students with a near fifty-fifty racial balance. Tuition was $580 per year (or roughly three thousand in 2019 dollars). Teacher salaries were three thousand dollars (or fifteen hundred in 2019 dollars). Even though the tuition seemed low, close to half the students were receiving financial aid (something that remains true to this day at Crossroads). The bottom line is that we really could have used a voucher system in which students did not have to pay tuition and in which teacher salaries had been more livable.

What was unique about Crossroads? Many things, but here are two that stand out. First, we actively sought to be a racially integrated school. Second, we looked for students and teachers who could live with the following philosophy: If teachers treat students with respect and dignity, then students have a responsibility to do the same with one another and with the teachers. I'm fairly confident in saying that overall, it worked well.

One of the interesting things about independent schools such as Crossroads is that they can be experimental. In fact, they can be whimsical when helpful to students' learning. I remember in Crossroads' first year (1974-75), we had an eighth-grade student named Keith who was roundly loved. However, he started not showing up for school for no explicable reason. I was teaching a class, I think it was Algebra, and the twelve students in the class expressed their frustration to me that Keith was not there. So, I said that if he won't come to us, let's go to him.

I packed the students into our fifteen-passenger Dodge van and we drove over to Keith's house in a somewhat sketchy part of town. We got out of the van, went to the front door, and one of the students rang the doorbell. Keith answered, and he looked stunned standing there in his pajamas.

I asked him if we could have class in the largest room of his home. He was a bit embarrassed, but he said yes. We went ahead and had class.

Keith's attendance after our home visit was not perfect, but in the vernacular of public school report cards, he "showed improvement." Regardless, it was an experience that all of us enjoyed and certainly remember. This is the kind of thing that you can do in a school that is based on informality and empathy.

The very same year that Crossroads began (1974), forced busing to promote racial integration began in the city of St. Louis. Within a decade, the program expanded to include nearly two dozen independent districts in St. Louis County, something that dramatically increased the number of students in the area who attended racially integrated schools.

I am not going to try to assess how well the voluntary

desegregation program went and any macro analysis overlooks the fact that there were hundreds of thousands of individual students involved and each one had his or her own experiences in the program. What I will say is there could have been a different way to promote racial integration in St. Louis, and elsewhere.

The problem of segregated schools has gotten worse in recent years. More than sixty years after the *Brown v. Board of Education* Supreme Court decision, our public schools are more segregated in every region of the country except the West than they were in 1980. Very little court-ordered desegregation remains. Utilizing vouchers to integrate would provide new opportunities for families that value integration to ensure that their students could attend integrated schools. The key would be that schools could not discriminate.

Working with young, idealistic teachers, dozens of new independent schools could be established, reflecting a basic commitment to ensuring that student bodies are racially integrated. These schools could be located throughout the metropolitan area, providing opportunities for students to go to integrated schools close to home or in a distant venue if they preferred. The schools would not be cookie-cutter; they could have varying curricula, largely developed by each school's teachers. They could be relatively small in size, making the relations between teachers, students and parents much stronger.

This was a dream that I had when starting Crossroads, and still have. I love the idea of new schools constantly being created, powered by the vision of young teachers who are energetic and want to focus on the totality of each child's needs. However, for all the reasons previously stated, we are currently in a political climate that prohibits this from happening. Good ideas need to first become part of the national dialogue before they can be implemented. Mega-kudos to former Congressman Dennis Kucinich and John Conyers, as well as Senator Bernie Sanders who tenaciously worked to make the concept of Medicare-for-All an essential part of our national conversation on health care. We are coming closer and closer to making this idea, or some hybrid form of it, a reality. Hopefully that can happen in the future with a voucher program that only includes schools which do not discriminate.

The United States could not jump into vouchers tomorrow any more than it could immediately begin to model empathy. But we have to start somewhere and be patient. Schools are perhaps more important to the character of the nation than we realize. Conservatives get enormous benefits from school systems that discourage the questioning of authority. Those students who are not confident to question authority in school are unlikely to question it in their governmental leaders. Progressives have much to gain, as does the general population, if our schools can become better models of empathy and less of automatic compliance with authority.

If there is one number in this book to remember, it is ten thousand—the number of hours that students spend in schools in grades K12. If they are characterized by boredom, adherence to all authority, and learning by rote, we will not have an inquisitive and responsive body politic. We need to change what we do in schools so that there is more independent, creative and critical thinking. We need to have empathy flowing back and forth between teachers and students. If we can do this, future generations will have much better chances of providing our country with the leaders that we need and deserve.

Chapter 4

WHAT OUR SURVEY AND FOCUS GROUP TELL US ABOUT INTROVERTS AND POLITICS

W HAT WOULD IT take to motivate an introverted non-voter to cast a ballot?

"If we were literally going to war… and they counted everybody's vote and it was like a war issue or I die, then that would motivate me," said one of our eight participants in a focus group made up of self-identified introverts who had at least two years of college and who had not voted in the past two presidential elections.

This educated participant was also asked, "If one candidate supports programs to help people who are economically struggling and the other candidate supports giving tax breaks to the wealthy, would you be motivated to vote?" She replied, "It's never prompted me to vote before."

If we talk about changing how America votes by getting previous non-voters to the ballot box, there are two numbers for us to keep in mind. The first is ninety-two **million**—that's the number of eligible citizens who did not vote in the presidential election of 2016. The second number is forty percent—that's the percentage of the 235 million citizens who could vote but did not.

In the best of worlds, these ninety-two million citizens would decide to vote, and they would make their decisions based on empathy and critical thinking. Perhaps, we would no longer have to suffer presidencies like Nixon, G.W. Bush or Trump. But it's not that simple; each and every one of those ninety-two million has his or her own reason for not voting. For some, they are suppressed from getting to the polls, but for most it is a decision of their own volition.

To learn more about ways in which we can jump-start efforts to activate voters who are empathetic and use critical thinking skills, we conducted a wide-spread survey of over one thousand respondents. We were looking for patterns of who voted and who didn't. We also looked for any correlations between voting and persons who lean towards being introverted or ranking high on a scale of empathy.

Our survey and focus group findings were not conclusive, but there are strong indicators that there are ways to draw more people to the polls and specifically to draw those people who value empathy and critical thinking.

First, the results from the focus group:

Each participant wants the Electoral College to be abolished. The E.C. is a major deterrent to many people voting. These non-voters simply believe that their votes don't count because they don't have a real say in the election.

The eight participants agree that there is far too much money in politics. They would be comfortable with eliminating private contributions and replacing them with publicly-funded campaigns.

If "the system" could do one thing for non-voters, it would be to provide them with clear, unbiased, encapsulated nuggets of information about issues and candidates. Many non-voters do not trust what they receive from either candidates or the mainstream media. They would like objective information, available to them in a variety of forms so that each potential voter could find an appropriate reading level and degree of complexity to investigate material. The medium for the information could be printed or digital, whatever is most comfortable to each citizen.

Those who see themselves as introverts and who are fairly well-educated non-voters want better choices of candidates. They find too many current candidates to be "in-your-face" and not at all like them. They prefer candidates who brag less and with whom they would be comfortable having a beer or a quiet conversation at a coffee house. Many wanted to vote against Donald Trump, but felt that Hillary Clinton was inauthentic.

They would like shorter, quieter campaigns. Current campaigns are simply "too loud." They send too much high-volume stimulation to voters for too long a period of time. It is easy for skeptical voters to simply tune it out.

They want candidates to live by similar standards to those they set for themselves. In their somewhat quiet ways, they strive to be as authentic as possible. They want more candidates who seem "real" to them; who still maintain the personal core of who they were when they were younger and not running for office.

A lot of these voters feel as if they are getting punched in the gut by the political process. They are not respected, and the campaigns come across as assaults. They want campaigns to be toned down.

Most members of the group try to avoid going to unnecessary social engagements. But I asked them if they would be willing to go to a party across the street or a bar-be-que down the block if there was a well-known person there who they would like to meet. Most said yes. It was interesting who they suggested as people they would like to meet: actor Will Smith, former Secretary of State Colin Powell and the Kennedys. Will Smith has been identified as an introvert as has Colin Powell. Bobby Kennedy, in particular, was uncomfortable putting on an "extrovert hat" and campaigning, but he did it when he had to because he knew that he could not be elected without doing so.

Most of the participants in the focus group indicated that for them to seriously consider voting, candidates would first have to change. They are looking for a new breed of candidates. Currently, anyone who takes the plunge to run for office essentially has to turn their life upside down, sacrificing their lease on privacy. They go from one demanding social event to another. They sit for hours dialing for dollars, acting like glorified beggars and inevitably indebting themselves to whomever will respond to their query with a favor.

These are things that introverts don't do. They prefer quiet, less stressful ways of spending their time. They are more likely to value time to reflect, to consider more than one side to an issue, to try to hang on to their inner-selves as they navigate their way through the days. That inner-self is who they want to go home to at night when they recharge their batteries.

These are people who we need to bring into the political arena, and people such as those in our focus group who have chosen not to vote may be among the first to lend their support to more reserved and refined candidates.

We also learned from the group that they had varying degrees of government and current events studies while in school. Some had learned quite a bit but felt that what they learned discouraged them from trusting the system. Their current comfort zone is to not participate, either because they see the system as corrupt or because they feel that the issues are too complicated to master.

The focus group gives us strong indicators that some introverts think that the political system does not connect well with them. As we discussed issues, I had a sense that if these citizens did vote, they likely would have leaned left. Keep in mind that the focus group may have been somewhat stacked in that direction because they were generally well-educated, and we know that the more educated an individual is, the more likely they are to vote Democrat[13].

In our survey of over a thousand people, we did not screen respondents for their educational levels.

The most dramatic finding was that extroverts are twelve percent more likely to vote in presidential elections (fifty-nine to forty-seven percent). Extroverts are even more likely to vote in non-presidential elections (forty to twenty-three percent). Introverts far more likely fall into the categories of "seldom voters" and "non-voters." These figures should not be surprising from what we learned from our focus group. Introverts are more readily turned off by all the hoopla and banality of most campaigns. Even going to the polls can sometimes be stressful. A good way to make voting more

---

13   https://www.pewresearch.org/fact-tank/2018/11/08/the-2018-midterm-vote-divisions-by-race-gender-education/

acceptable and accessible would be for more states to adopt vote-by-mail, a system that is currently in place in Colorado, Oregon, and Washington state.

When it comes to going door-to-door asking people to support a candidate of their choice, or making phone calls on behalf of a candidate, we found that only three percent of introverts were comfortable doing that compared to sixteen percent of extroverts.

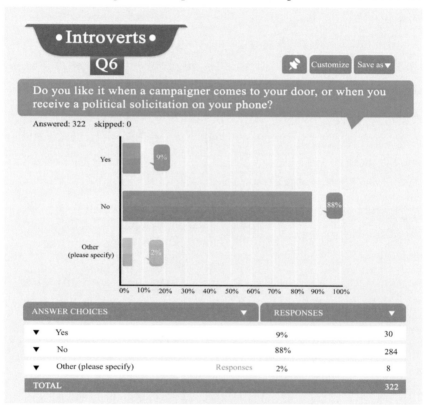

And while thirty percent of extroverts like it when a campaigner comes to their door, or when they receive a political solicitation, only nine percent of introverts do. Eighty-eight percent of introverts clearly do not like it, compared to sixty-six percent of extroverts.

Regarding political persuasions, we did find that introverts did lean more to the left than extroverts. Among introverts, Democrats outnumbered Republicans thirty-four to twenty-nine percent. For extroverts, it was forty-one to thirty-eight percent Republican. This is not a huge difference, but it is an indicator that it might be wise

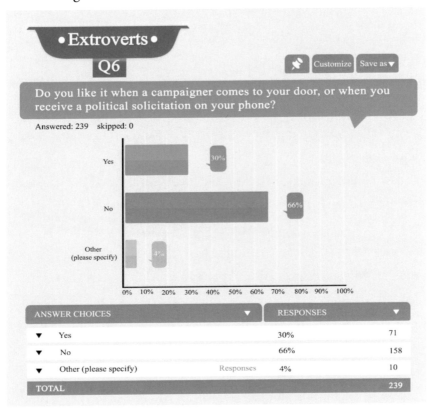

for Democrats to appeal more to introverts and Republicans more to extroverts.

We asked questions that gave indicators as to whether or not a person might rank high on empathy. The bellwether question was, "If a person is poor, which **two** of the factors listed below do you think explain why that person is poor? Please select all that apply:

The person is lazy.

The person has not received a good education.

The person would prefer to be on welfare.

The person has faced a lot of hardships in their life.

None of the above.

Clearly the empathetic answers are b) and d); the non-empathetic as answers being a) and c). Among those who gave empathetic answers, thirty-nine percent were Democrats and thirty-two percent Republicans. The gap is much greater for those who believe someone is poor because of laziness or would prefer to be on welfare, fifty-three percent Republican to twenty-one percent Democrat.

The results of the survey and the focus group were not startling. The differences between introverts and extroverts, and those who measured high and low on the empathy scales were not dramatic. But they were significant enough to give anyone who wants to see voter turnout increase, particularly among individuals who mainly lean left, validation to consider different strategies in the selection of candidates and the ways in which campaigns are run. It would particularly behoove Democrats to tone down their appeals to at least a segment of voters.

What can candidates do to attract more empathetic, introverted people to vote?

This is a tough question, but central to how the type of reform we want can come about.

Perhaps the most desirable way would be to have candidates who themselves tend to be introverted. There is a conundrum with this because the nature of current politics repels people who are more reserved. The way to draw more political introverts into running for office is three-fold: (a) structural changes in the system such as reducing the length of campaigns; (b) for politically introverted voters, in their own ways, to let potential introverted candidate know that they, the voters, would like them to run; and (c) for the media to acknowledge that some candidates prefer to have more subdued campaigns and their increased participation in politics will elevate the level and quality of political dialogue.

All candidates can dial down their intensity. Backing off of negative ads is a good way to start. Offering more town halls as an alternative to political rallies would increase the comfort level for political introverts. Appearing at fewer events so that one seems fresher and less rehearsed would provide more authenticity to voters.

Clearly spell out views on issues. Do not overgeneralize or present obvious inconsistencies. Avoid hypocrisy. If a candidate really cares about the issues, convey that commitment to reform is more important than winning the race.

Work with campaign staff to communicate directly with individual voters, utilizing social media, and whenever possible, old-fashioned emails even letters to let voters know that you are listening.

Many candidates will not be capable of making these changes. But for those who can, and who desire to, there may be a very positive pay-off in bringing new voters into the fold, ones who are looking for authenticity and want genuine communication rather than loud noise.

Chapter 5

CANDIDATES AND VOTERS – INTROVERTS ON THE OUTSIDE

W E ALL KNOW what it's like to leave our home to drive somewhere and suddenly remember that we forgot our car keys. That's one kind of a mistake. Here's a bigger whopper. The San Francisco Giants were building a new baseball stadium scheduled to open in April 2000, but they forgot something. The architects and engineers had failed to include the bullpens for the relief pitchers. Seems hard to believe, but it's true. They were forced to jerry-rig the stadium and put the bullpens between the foul lines and the grandstands. The solution worked, but the oversight meant that relief pitchers did not have, and still do not have, a place to stretch, play light catch, and mentally psych themselves for the game.

Similar errors of omission happen in politics. What if a candidate forgets an entire bloc of voters? Seemingly that would be catastrophic, but in contemporary America, it's possible to win using the strategy of "divide and conquer" the electorate. So long as a party can cobble together a plurality of the voters, it does not matter whether that plurality is constructed from homogeneous voters (likely Republican) or a collection of heterogeneous groups (more likely Democrat). Getting more votes than anyone else is the name of the game in current politics.

After the 2012 elections, the Republican Party made a pledge to become more inclusive by reaching out to minorities and women. The effort was tepid, and it failed. Four years later, Donald Trump figured out a way to light a fire under the Archie Bunkers of the world and the GOP was able to patch together enough voters to win the presidential election of 2016 by appealing to its traditional base "on steroids."

Democrats are often called the party of identity politics. The Party tries to create coalitions out of disparate parts that, under ideal circumstances, are seamlessly patched together in a quilt-like manner. Add one part women, another part African-Americans, another part eighteen to thirty-year olds, and a few other distinct groups, and the coalition should be solid. Unfortunately for Democrats, in 2016, there were not enough of each group to win a majority. Furthermore, the coalition was rough around the edges and struggled with in-fighting. The Democrats were hurt by Trump having an uncanny awareness of the needs of many white people, particularly those with limited education. In 2016, many in the traditional base of the Democratic Party either stayed home and did not vote, or actually, as was the case of eleven percent of 2012 Obama voters, chose to vote for Trump.

Every successful election for Democrats requires the party to pull together disparate groups to gather a plurality of the votes. The more effective that they can be in including the maximum number of patches from a mosaic quilt of minorities, the better they will do at the polls. Republicans are also going to have to learn how to attract better minorities, because they are running against the clock. They only have until 2045 before white people no longer represent a majority of Americans[14].

If you are a traditional candidate from either major party in the U.S., you want to generate maximum possible turnout from your base, from those who identify with you and think that you are a good candidate. While turning out your base is often the key to victory, each candidate has an enormous reservoir of potential votes that rarely get tapped—the forty percent of Americans who do not vote in presidential elections. For non-presidential elections, the number can jump up to sixty percent.

Similar to the Democratic Party, the non-voters are diverse. Some are simply apathetic. Some feel that their votes don't matter. Others fear doing anything that involves interacting with a government agency, even those as un-intimidating as the workers at polling places. Many citizens want to vote but can't, often due to restrictions imposed upon them by state governments and federal court rulings.

There is another big group which is rarely identified—people who see themselves at political introverts. They too are not a monolith. A significant number of these political introverts are non-voters. Among those, some are also apathetic; some feel alienated; others think it makes no sense to vote. Our research has shown that many find the whole presidential election system to be tainted because in many states the Electoral College completely undermines the concept of one person, one vote.

What many political introverts have in common with one another is frustration with those in the political class who bloviate,

---

14   https://www.brookings.edu/blog/the-avenue/2018/03/14/the-us-will-become-minority-white-in-2045-census-projects/

who speak without thinking and who rarely let another person get

Carol Ruzicka

a word in edgewise. Many political introverts do not suffer fools gladly. All this adds up to a large bloc of voters who are not attracted to loud political candidates, and that's a large number. While these potential voters make a choice to not have their voices heard in elections, the candidates who do not recognize their presence run the risk of losing these potential voters.

On occasion, there are political introverts "who can't take it any longer" and break out of their shells to become the most persuasive of political activists. No one exemplifies this better than Greta Thunberg, the seventeen-year-old Swedish environmental activist who single-handedly raised the world's attention to the need for today's adults to address climate change for the sake of future generations. What started as skipping school on Fridays to protest in front of the Swedish Parliament became an international movement with millions of students and adults pressuring their governments and the United Nations to act with immediacy. This cannot be too easy for her as an introvert, but she could no longer tolerate seeing the world burn up while she did nothing.

To the degree that a candidate is aware of political introverts who are not regular voters, he or she is presented with opportunities. These opportunities are for both the candidate and the voter, the way it should be.

If a candidate wishes to expand her voting base by appealing to political introverts who do not regularly vote, she has decisions to make. A thorough cost-benefit analysis would identify whether picking up the votes of political introverts outweighs the possible loss of the votes of some political extroverts. If there is a trade-off, what is best for the candidate, picking up some introverts or not losing some extroverts?

I would argue that it is better for candidates, voters and the country as a whole for candidates to try harder to connect with politically introverted voters. Here are some reasons why:

Introverts are often thoughtful and frequently empathetic as well. While not a rule, data substantiates this contention. In her book *The Introvert Advantage: How Quiet People Can Thrive in an Extrovert World*, Marti Olsen Laney suggests that many good ideas come from the minds of introverts and are implemented by extroverts.

Political introverts quiet down campaigns. The less noise, the more opportunity to elevate and expand the conversation, to focus on the country's needs rather than spectacle of the current campaign circus.

Our research shows that self-identified political introverts are more likely to align with the Democratic Party. Introverts also like exchanges of ideas. If either party is going to be more open to dialogue, the Democratic Party is most likely.

Our political system frequently works poorly, and this may be because our society is frequently characterized by discombobulated and dysfunctional behavior. Collectively, we are fragmented as we have rarely been. Income disparity is growing and politically we are more segmented than we have been since the Gilded Age. Trying to fix politics without trying to change the collective values and habits of the voters is a non-starter, akin to trying to clean up the global environment without first addressing local pollution. We can only fix our political process as we simultaneously improve who we are individually and collectively as human beings.

There are plenty of stories about how ill-informed the American electorate is. According to Forbes, only about thirty-four percent of

Americans can name the three branches of the federal government: executive, legislative and judicial[15].

Only one in one thousand Americans can name the five freedoms laid out in the First Amendment: speech, religion, press, assembly and petition[16].

Some sixth graders were recently asked to pick their favorite **countries**. Among the suggestions were Hollywood and New York.

Forbes Magazine has noted:

"Some learn about politics for reasons other than voting. Just as sports fans follow sports because they like rooting for their favorite team, "political fans" follow politics because they enjoy cheering on their favorite political "team." Committed partisans usually know a lot more about politics than the average voter. But they evaluate that information in a highly biased way, overvaluing anything that supports their preexisting views and devaluing or ignoring that which cuts against them. Political fans also tend to discuss politics only with those who agree with their views. They follow it mainly through like-minded media. We are a nation of people living in bubbles[17]."

It does not take a rocket scientist to conclude that if you have poorly informed and unmotivated voters, you'll likely get a large number of politicians hovering near the lowest common denominator.

------

15   https://www.forbes.com/sites/jaredmeyer/2016/06/27/american-voters-are-ignorant-but-not-stupid/#183e2af07ff1
16   https://wallstreetinsanity.com/10-facts-americans-dont-know-about-american-politics-history-and-basic-knowledge/
17   https://www.forbes.com/sites/realspin/2014/11/03/what-no-one-talks-about-during-election-season-voter-ignorance/#8fd2b0fa4946

One of the underlying principles of effecting change in politics is for people to respond to a "call to action." What exactly does this mean? Most particularly, what does a call to action mean for someone who considers him or herself to be an introvert?

There is a disconnect between a call to action and asking an introvert to follow the call. It is somewhat oxymoronic to think of an introvert yelling and shouting to friends to join a movement. Candidates running traditional campaigns will have as much success trying to get introverts to volunteer and engage as if they were trying to tear down a steel door with a toothpick. It won't work.

So, if a candidate decides that he wants to attract political introverts to his campaign, he's going to have to try techniques that are thoroughly different from the intense techniques he uses to attract extroverts or other political junkies.

Those who are more extroverted contribute to campaigns in two traditional ways. The first is to work for the candidate. This often involves the ground game: knocking on doors, making phone calls, distributing yard signs, going to rallies and other gatherings. All these contributions involve a large investment in time. If someone has that time, it may be acceptable, but the question should be asked, "does this kind of work do anything to elevate the conversation of the campaign?" or," does it make fellow citizens more aware of any reasons a candidate is suitable for office?" These can be difficult questions to answer, but certainly worth asking.

The second way to give is financially. Most campaigns are propelled by large donations. This makes the system biased towards those who have the financial means to invest in political campaigns.

Candidates and their staffs have gotten wiser in recent years and now try to supplement their large donations with a lot of small ones from individual donors. Raising three million dollars by way of one hundred thousand donations of thirty dollars is much more powerful than three donations of one million each because each of the one hundred thousand donors now have a vested interest in the campaign. Their power at the ballot box is much greater than the three who gave a million dollars each.

When Bernie Sanders ran for president in 2016, he was proud to claim that his average donation was twenty-seven dollars. This was in considerable contrast to Hillary Clinton who was the darling of the SuperPACS, PACs, and the Glitterati.

Paid for by Bernie 2020

(not the billionaires)

Bernie essentially started a new movement in which it became much easier for an individual to give a small amount. Utilizing the internet in ways that even Barack Obama had not institutionalized, he and others gave voters the opportunity to donate as little as one dollar to the cause. A solicitation would look like this:

"Can you make a $3 donation to help me rally progressives to vote ahead of this election and in support of our progressive agenda? We are winning, and that's because of support from people like you[18]."

---

18   https://secure.actblue.com/donate/bernie-october?akid=289.420771.
XEP1al&rd=1&refcode=em181029-full&refcode2=289_420771_XEP1al&t=25

If you contribute three dollars, it creates a feeling that you are "one of many." Other like-minded people are joining the cause with you and together you create change. But possibly unbeknownst to you, as soon as you give that first dollar or first three dollars, you are on their list forever. Your name on the list is like a cell in a virus. It spreads until there is no other place to go, and for all we know, it may wind up in Moscow. You thought you were giving to only one candidate, but in reality, your contact information is shared with a whole group of candidates and causes that are interlocked in a fund-raising cabal.

ADD YOUR NAME

If you don't mind getting email or snail mail solicitations all the time, then the system may work for you. It is possible that you have a sense of identity in a political community, where you are part of an effort to help someone with whom you identify win. You may even advance concerns that are important to you.

But how big is the universe of people who give money to candidates or who go door-to-door asking for support? Recent data shows that only four percent of the electorate volunteer on political or issue campaigns and five percent donate money to a political or issues campaign[19]. Only four percent attend political rallies, another major form of building support for a candidate or cause.

Many people may prefer a more passive form of involvement. More than eighteen million people tuned in to the Democratic

---

19   https://www.theatlantic.com/business/archive/2014/05/only-one-percent-of-americans-are-really-politically-active/425286/

presidential debates on both June 26 and 27, 2019 and another nine million live-streamed[20]. That's close to half of the total who voted for Hillary Clinton in 2016. Thoughtful, albeit loud, debates and forums may be the way to go. Quiet, round-table forums might be even better.

I ran for Congress twice, in 2010 and 2014. Both times I was the underdog and the Republican candidates chose to take a pass on candidate forums sponsored by the League of Women Voters. But as the Democratic candidate, I was fortunate that each time a thoughtful Libertarian joined me on the panel. We covered considerable ground in ninety minutes without any yelling and screaming, only consideration of the issues. I understand why the Republicans chose not to participate. Not because they were afraid of me, but because of the political axiom that debates are risky for front runners. But the voters were the real losers. They did not get a chance to see if the Republicans could defend their positions with opposition, or at least questioning individuals, in the room. One very special thing that the League did was to not allow clapping or any form of audience intrusion. These forums were not part of a high-tech, high-distraction circus; they were thoughtful considerations of important issues. Audience feedback was overwhelmingly positive.

Those who engage in the big three of volunteering, donating, and going to rallies get a disproportionate amount of the goodies from our political system. But a key question is, "Are citizen volunteers 'selling' candidates the best way for the United States to meet its public needs? Would it be better to minimize the salesmanship and

---

20   https://www.cnn.com/2019/06/28/media/nbc-democratic-debate-ratings-night-two/index.html

maximize candidates and voters brainstorming solutions to our challenges?"

What do we know about the vast majority who don't volunteer, donate or go to rallies and why don't they? We know that some are apathetic, but many others care deeply about remedying America's problems. They may have very good reasons to not actively engage in political campaigns.

Their lives are full; they don't have time to engage in this kind of politics.

They see a low return on personal investment in politics.

They don't have the money to donate.

They are not satisfied with the candidates.

They don't like to be part of a group or herd mentality.

Buyer beware; they really don't know what they are getting when they hitch up with a candidate or cause.

There is uncertainty as to what happens next, especially with disclosure of information that they might prefer to keep private.

They don't like having something as important as politics being so much like celebrity "show and tell."

They don't like the harsh imbalance of power between candidates and voters.

A key point in this book is to look at the dichotomy that we have between those who actively engage in politics and those who don't. A considerable part of this difference is revealed through the distinctions between those among us who are more extroverted and those who are more introverted. It may make our conversations easier to understand if we simply refer to some of us as being extroverted and others introverted, but we should keep in mind that there is an extrovert-introvert continuum and each of us sits somewhere along it. More accurately, each of us moves along the continuum, but we each have comfort zones that define where on the continuum we spend the preponderance of our time.

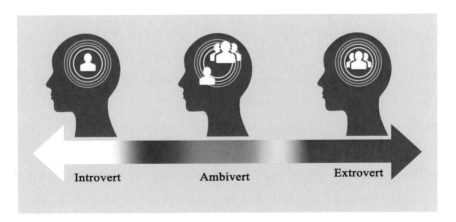

As we have seen, our political system is biased in favor of those who lean towards being extroverted rather than those who lean introverted. In order to succeed in politics, most candidates have historically needed to be extroverted, which often entails meeting new people, being in crowds, asking for money and other favors, and being the center of attention. This also describes their most fervent supporters. Many who work on campaigns like mixing with the public, arranging social gatherings, and engaging in the rough and tumble of politics. Yes, there are some who work from home, engaging in data entry or other valuable kinds of work distanced from crowds. But at the very least, those who are comfortable knocking on the doors of strangers are a unique brand of people. They may not be as assertive as Mormons or Jehovah's Witnesses who knock on your door and try to convert your religious beliefs, but they don't mind engaging in a way that can be very off-putting to others. One has to wonder if their door-knocking actually helps the candidate for whom they are working or hurts them because so many people find the knock to be a rude intrusion.

It's hard to know how our society breaks down in terms of extroverts and introverts. Caroline Beaton reports in *Psychology Today* that the two terms were devised by Carl Jung in the 1920s[21]. Jung described extroverts as drawing energy from their surroundings and relationships whereas introverts draw it from being alone. But he conceded, that "There is, finally, a third group, and here it is hard to say whether the motivation comes chiefly from with or without." He said that this group is the most numerous; ones who are neither extroverts nor introverts. They are now called ambiverts—people with balanced, nuanced personalities composed of both introverted and extroverted traits.

What is important to note is that political extroverts, like political introverts, are a minority of the population. So, to the extent that our political system and process is geared towards extroverts, candidates would do well to make special appeals to those in the center of the continuum, as well as those who are introverted.

The fact that politics is geared towards extroverts does not make it different from other activities in our popular culture. We are constantly being assaulted by stimuli at ramped up levels that are almost impossible for many human beings to take. Have you gone to a movie recently and sat through the trailers? Have you gone to a professional sporting event at a major league venue? It's almost

---

21   https://www.psychologytoday.com/us/blog/the-gen-y-guide/201710/
the-majority-people-are-not-introverts-or-extroverts

wall-to-wall assault. The louder the better. The brighter the better. With the movies, the scarier and the gorier, the better. That may do the trick for some, but there are many who want the stimulation toned down.

With the growth of electronic assaults, politics has become more and more like loud sporting events. We all know that Trump rallies in many ways are hate-fests. Democratic rallies also do a fair amount of demonizing. What proportion of the American people enjoy attending one of these humongous political gatherings?

Let's step back for a moment and remember what politics is supposed to be. Politics is the sum of all the activities associated with selecting the governing leaders of our society. The decisions we make as citizens are significant, in fact they are more important than who wins American Idol, The Voice, and every other reality-show iteration. Most politicians are like costumed characters at Mardi Gras, wearing a series of masks. What you see on the surface is hardly who they really are. You can peel off one piece of costume at a time, but it takes a long time until all the garish clothing and make-up is removed and all that remains is who the person really is.

When we judge politicians on how well they can whoop up a crowd, how gently they kiss a baby, how in-stride they walk in a parade, we know virtually nothing about who they would be as a national or local leader. We have to remember that we get what we value. If it is more important to us for a politician to glad-hand with people at a bar-be-que than it is for them to be able to analyze issues and advance solutions to problems, then we get what we deserve. In many ways, we're looking at it now.

So much of what politicians do is shrouded in the money they raise. The money allows them to better hide behind an image they like to create—an image that embellishes who they really are and often demonizes their opponents.

Is it any small wonder that many Americans would prefer to have little or nothing to do with political campaigns? They can be too loud; too garish; too removed from the way in which civilized people relate to one another.

Many Americans also do not feel connected at all with the political process. Gary runs a dry cleaner in a Midwestern suburban strip-mall. He's sixty-eight-years-old and has not voted since Ronald Reagan was president. He really got turned off to politics with Bill Clinton. He didn't like what Clinton did with Monica Lewinsky in the Oval Office.

Nothing that he has seen since the Clinton days has encouraged him to become actively involved in politics. Getting involved is clearly not worth it for him.

Gary reminds us that many people live in bubbles when it comes to our political process. A big bubble in our country encompasses the millions of people who were never introduced to politics—and more importantly to public policy—at home or at school. It's tough to ask someone eighteen or older with little exposure to politics and public policy to look at political campaigns through the twin lenses of critical thinking and empathy.

Kelly has been working as a waitress at a popular delicatessen/ restaurant in a fairly wealthy suburb. Like Gary, she did not talk much about politics while in school. She took a Government and Politics class in high school, but contemporary issues were rarely discussed. She voted with some enthusiasm for Obama, but as the mother of three children, engaging in politics is just not a top priority.

Like Gary, Kelly wants politicians to be more in touch with people like herself: those who work intense jobs and don't have time to play around. Kelly reminds us that while many people say that the key to better politics is more candidates who are like "everyday people."

Some politicians try to selectively project that they are "one of the people," but among the people who they do not fool are most of the non-voters in America.

In their muted tones, political introverts hue and cry for politicians to notice them. They want candidates to speak to them about important issues, but in ways that match how they prefer non-politicians and other non-salespersons to address them: friend-to-friend, without pretense, and in a courteous and respectful professional manner. Political introverts would like to be spared the gross imbalance of power where the politician is someone special and they, the voter, is a peon. Instead of being shouted at during political rallies, they prefer the conversations of well-moderated town hall meetings.

Attracting political introverts requires a different type of candidate. For example:

Someone who is humble, without telling everyone that they are.

Someone concerned about issues, but not a yeller or screamer.

Someone willing to acknowledge when they do not know something and willing to find out the answer.

This one in particular requires the media to accept such an answer as reasonable and respectable. Often times, they demean a candidate who does not have an immediate answer. Someone who is a rational thinker and a problem solver.

Someone who is empathetic without being maudlin.

Someone who is able to see themselves as vulnerable and doesn't try to hide it.

Someone who is aware of the "imposter syndrome;" the idea that they may be faking it, trying to be someone who they are not. This is an asset; it goes with humility. It's healthy to admit that at times one is "winging it" and like everyone, is a "work in progress."

Someone who is willing to communicate with irony, recognizing that one is not an expert; that there are certain imponderables in life; that none of us has a corner on wisdom and there are times when we have to laugh at ourselves.

Someone who is comfortable without always having a camera within range. Someone who might have a campaign regulation: no selfies.

America is simply not used to candidates who run modest campaigns and aren't always shilling for money, or even votes. But for those politicians who embody these qualities and do a better job of communicating with political introverts, the first result is that a large group of individuals who may have been alienated from the world of politics may now be willing to engage. Equally important, attracting political introverts will bring more people into the political arena who are empathetic.

You might say that none of this can happen quickly. But it is important to recognize that there is a distinction between running and winning. Think of it this way. We're all familiar with the adage that you have to walk before you can run. Well if we're talking about political candidates who embody many of the characteristics listed above, in most cases, they have to run before they can win.

Successful modest campaigns are not common in America. But think of what you like in a friend. Is it someone who is begging from you? Probably not, and modesty is what the American people need to learn to value in political candidates, for when they are elected these candidates will be most sensitive to their individual and societal needs.

When I ran for Congress, I did not win; I didn't even come close (although I could manipulate some comparative statistics to make it look like I was really in the running). What I did do was (a) ensure that Democrats had a candidate in a very important race in a district they well may win six years after I last ran, and (b) let voters know (albeit a small universe of the voters in the district) that someone was running without asking for money and offering a platform that was entirely devoid of obligations to anyone else. In the League of Women candidate forums, I was able to answer difficult questions, hopefully without being defensive.

In the same district in 2018, a political science professor from St. Louis Community College at Meramec, John Messmer, ran a similar campaign. He was much more effective than me in finding venues in which to speak and his detailed platform was a "no excuses" one that covered a wide range of difficult issues. He went deep into the weeds describing the many structural changes that are needed in American politics. He shed light on difficult issues, and his candor and familiarity with issues stood him very well in the League forum among five Democrats running in the primary. John did not win, but again, he made voters aware of the fact that every candidate does not have to be about so-called heroism or glitz or galas or dollars. The voters in Missouri's Second District are much wiser because of his effort.

A symbiotic relationship exists between enlarging the voting pool to include more introverts and getting different kinds of candidates to run for office. Currently, it is surprising to many voters when they learn of a candidate who keeps a "brag-free" zone around herself. But as more candidates take that tact, the wins will start piling up.

We have to do something different. Virtually all of us who have ever gone to school have heard that "the future of the world is up to your generation." It's not that no one listened when that was being said, but with the proof being in the pudding, no generation has really been an agent of the necessary changes to move our society forward in a dramatic and sustainable way. If any of us had, we would not have Donald Trump as president with over thirty-five percent of the adult population, no matter how legitimate their grievances, choosing to lend their support to Trump.

As we said in the last chapter, our schools have the greatest opportunity to affect change. For our schools to change, they have to focus more on critical thinking and empathy. They must attract/ employ different kinds of teachers; ones who are not afraid to challenge authority and conventional wisdom. They must not have their minds programmed by professional education schools; rather they should be as close as possible in touch with their inner child and that of their students. This is all part of the process of making politics more welcoming to political introverts and ultimately having government work better for all of us.

Chapter 6
REPUBLICAN & DEMOCRATIC BRAINS

THERE IS NOT a word in the Constitution about political parties. Our first president, George Washington, warned against them. But by the time our second president, John Adams, took office the country had divided into parties, or clans, or teams, one called the Federalists (Adams); the other called the Democratic-Republicans (Thomas Jefferson).

Many consider political parties to be the death knell of our democracy. But it's hard to imagine a nation addressing its disagreements over public policy without people aligning themselves into groups; each trying to advance its own agenda.

The problem in the United States is that we have only two major parties and they currently seem to be in a perpetual state of gridlock. They spend considerable time demonizing one another, particularly the Republican Party where fear and even hatred seem to drive the agenda. Democrats have their own fervor and even irrationality from time to time.

Each party seems to live within the confines of a wall, or at best, a semi-permeable barrier. While each seeks to invite new voters into its party, neither seems hospitable to those who nest on the outside. Specifically, political introverts have little inclination to knock on a forbidding door and join a noisy circus. To the extent that political introverts care about or are involved in politics, they prefer it not to be acrimonious, and with a minimum of demonizing. Political introverts who currently do not vote have potential to be helpful to either party, but few party insiders properly value nor know how to attract them.

When politics is solely about winning elections, and not public policy, government is not responsive to the needs of the citizens. At the Congressional level, Democrats are now working at fashioning an agenda that addresses many of the economic, social and human rights issues of the population. But the party has not yet constructed a broad consensus for a progressive or even liberal candidate to have a good chance of winning the presidency. If the party wants to win, it will have to do a much better job of attracting voters who may not be part of the Trump base, but who feel much of the frustration of those in the base.

Members of each party have unique characteristics; ones that are more deeply ingrained in defining differences in our society. Currently, political allegiance is a better predictor of preferences than most other factors such as gender, race, income, and education. Over the past twenty years, if you want to know what magazines to which someone subscribes or the television shows he watches, allegiance to a political party is a better predictor than race, gender, age, sexual orientation, or any other factor.

The harsh differences between the ways in which Republicans and Democrats think is not limited to those most directly involved in politics. Our culture reflects the chasm. We are nowhere close to having common ground on issues such as gun control, abortion rights, immigration policy, or strengthening the economic safety net for those who are poor. From the inside, the divide looks like gridlock. From the outside, it looks forbidding, and that is part of the reason why so many political introverts are reluctant to try to become active in either of the tribes.

Republicans have been digging in their heels ever since the bi-partisan era of the eighties when President Ronald Reagan (R) and Speaker of the House Tip O'Neill (D) had a warm personal relationship and successfully collaborated on legislation. They are the architects of our current political gridlock and their lack of empathy makes it easy for them to subscribe to the "politics of 'NO.'" But signs of extreme Republican obstinance had appeared as far back as the fifties in the era of Joe McCarthy. Their intransigence ramped up considerably with Barry Goldwater running for president in 1964 and has become more entrenched in the fifty-five years since as they've elevated to party leadership positions the likes of Richard Nixon, Pat Buchanan, Dan Quayle, Sarah Palin, George W. Bush, Dick Cheney, and Donald Trump.

From the progressive perspective, there are certain dysfunctions in our system that clearly are a result of conservative policies. Much of this has to do with conservatives' inflexibility to change, such as recognizing the shifting demographics in the country. Coupled with this is the intense feeling of dislike and even hatred that many conservatives direct at others who are not like them. But progressives also bear a large measure of responsibility when it comes to accepting and reinforcing a system that is wedded to relics of the past; a system which alienates political introverts, some of the best minds that we could have in the world of politics and public service.

Liberals continue to support the perpetuation of the Electoral

College. Democrats do little to change the structurally undemocratic process for selecting candidates from the party (the primary system, balkanized among the states). Most only pay lip service to changing the reliance on big money to fund campaigns. Finally, they continue to accept a campaign system that is so intense and work-intensive that it undermines a candidate's personal and family life, and makes it virtually impossible for political introverts, with the strengths that they bring to the table, to run for office.

Perhaps the clearest way to view the Republican Brain is through the lens of how the GOP responded to the election of Barack Obama in 2008. Obama stunned the nation, first by becoming the Democratic nominee for president, and then by defeating the formidable Senator John McCain in the general election. America had elected its first African-American president, but Obama was far more than a symbolic member of America's most oppressed minority (along with Native Americans). He was a remarkable man—scholarly, visionary, and committed to using reason and empathy to advance the quality of life of America, both domestically and as a neighbor in global affairs.

The path for an African-American to be elected president was long and arduous. Only forty years prior to Obama being elected, the United States Congress passed a remarkable law that essentially eliminated discrimination in the selling and renting of homes. President Lyndon Johnson proudly signed it. Three years prior to that, Washington passed a sweeping Voting Rights Act that authorized federal registrars to oversee voting districts (primarily in the South) where there had been systematic discrimination against equal voting rights for African-Americans. The year prior to that

(1964), a sweeping public accommodations civil rights bill passed which outlawed discrimination against minorities in retail outlets and a host of other businesses.

When Obama won in 2008, many thought that America was moving into a post-racial period, particularly in politics. In many parts of America, he received a majority of the white vote. Caucasians had played vital roles in his campaign, both in his brain trust and also at the grassroots level, knocking on doors and working to convince others that "the time had come." And as might be expected, whites supplied the bulk of the money for his costly but well-financed campaigns.

What numerous progressives did not realize was how offensive the idea of an Obama presidency, or perhaps the idea of any African-American presidency, was to many of those who were not part of the "progressive team," particularly less-educated and economically strapped white people. Liberal Democrats were ready to move ahead, with ideas for advances that would both help them personally and society as a whole. A key legislative priority in the new agenda would be passage of some form of universal, affordable health care. Hadn't the electorate of 2008 given a mandate for such action?

Progressives operated in many ways as if the election of Barack Obama had moved the American political needle so far to the left that conservatives had been put in a corner and were going to stay largely silent for a while. Not only had Republicans lost a seminal election, but there also was the sense of dignity and propriety associated with Obama's election which gave it special significance. Obama supporters expected at least a nominal sense of respect from other Americans, considering that this was the election of our first African-American president. Now that the country had elected its first African-American president, didn't all citizens have a responsibility to give him all reasonable respect?

If Obama were to fail, wouldn't it be best for non-progressives to keep their hands clean while Rome burned? If someone were offended by an Obama presidency, shouldn't they have confidence in their own ideas and happily watch as the president self-imploded over a short measure of time?

But that is not what happened. Conservatives had no such patience. Instead they had a voracious appetite to undermine and destroy. Throughout American history, many pre-cursors pointed to what Republicans would do upon Obama's election. But nothing better forecast the party's tactics than their treatment of Hillary Clinton just ten years prior. In 1998, when her husband was under the scrutiny of Independent Prosecutor Kenneth Starr, Hillary Clinton referred to the opposition as being a "vast right-wing conspiracy," and she was right. It's unclear what she ever did wrong other than being a strong, thoughtful woman with an Ivy League pedigree who schmoozed with political bigwigs like almost every other politician. But Republicans and other conservatives put a big, fat target on her back and relentlessly took shots at her. It continues to this day with Trump rousing his crowds into the "Lock her up" chant.

Barack Obama had far fewer personal flaws than Hillary's husband, Bill, who served as president from 1993-2001. When adversity struck Obama about previous personal decisions such as his relationship with Reverend Jeremiah Wright in Chicago, he rationally assessed his options and then gave a strong speech in which he acknowledged possible mistakes on his part and accepted the ire that certain Americans had to the notion that he and Wright were close friends. Obama, along with Jimmy Carter thirty years earlier, showed that despite the fact that all of us err, some people, even in public life, are capable of maintaining a basic level of stability, sensitivity, and empathy.

Politics has now become the most divisive part of our society. The impact of the often-vicious conflict between parties extends well beyond the world of how we govern ourselves. It has become a better characterizer of our views on a wide range of issues including the environment, our recreational choices, the places we travel, the people with whom we socialize, the schools we attend and really how we view our fellow human beings.

This political polarization is not a secret. Many people blame it on both parties, saying that Democrats have moved much further to the left and Republicans to the right.

For more than a hundred years, Democrats have consistently maintained liberal positions except during a few periods such as the eighties when they bought into the Republican bullying that being liberal was unpatriotic. All the while, Republicans have been moving farther to the right.

If we look at American politics from the birth of the progressive era with Theodore Roosevelt (initially a Republican) at the beginning of the twentieth century, the original agendas are largely the same as those of contemporary progressives. There is a common denominator: to provide a safety net for all people who are at points in their lives where they cannot be self-sufficient.

Most of the legislative accomplishments of Democrats came during Franklin Roosevelt's New Deal and Lyndon Johnson's Great Society. The New Deal brought us acts such as the establishment of Social Security, the Wagner Act (vastly strengthening labor unions), job creation and economic recovery such as the Civilian Conservation Corps, Works Progress Administration Public Works Administration, Glass-Steagall Banking Act, the Federal Deposit Insurance Company, the Rural Electrification Administration, and the Tennessee Valley Authority.

There is a common denominator to all of these programs. They work to improve the quality of life for those who are struggling economically or with personal liberties.

Lyndon Johnson's Great Society provided a number of additional programs including Medicare and Medicaid, Head Start, Title I and other educational reforms, as well as dozens of other programs that addressed the domestic needs of the country.

Both the New Deal and Great Society were ended by wars. The New Deal ended as World War II brought a new type of prosperity with increased demand for products and elevated employment. The Great Society ended when Johnson lost his political base because he could not either "win the war in Vietnam" or extract the United States from the quagmire.

Fifty years after the Great Society, there is unfinished business in fabricating the safety net. Quite frankly, during the administrations of the past three Democratic presidents, Jimmy Carter, Bill Clinton, and Barack Obama, no legislation comparable to anything in the New Deal or Great Society was passed. Yes, the Affordable Care Act passed in 2010, but it was so diluted by Republican opposition that it did not even include the public option. Since its passage, it has unraveled from both political opposition and judicial restrictions.

What contemporary Democrats seek is essentially what most progressives through the years have wanted, beginning in the Teddy Roosevelt era. These include:

Job security

Income security

Universal affordable health care

Free and decent education for all

A clean environment

Civil rights and civil liberties for all

Consumer protection

There is very little that is radical about a society in which these rights and standards are the norm. The main argument against providing them is that "some people are getting something for nothing." But the premise of this line of thinking is that those who are currently wealthy have some "divine right" to be rich. Yes, there is a lot of history behind protecting and preserving the rights of the elite, the anointed, the elected. But since the Enlightenment of the eighteenth century, society has been moving more in the direction of recognizing the benefits of ensuring that everyone on this planet has a right to a decent life. This includes civil liberties and economic security.

Inevitably some people of modest means will fritter away what they have. But that is not an exclusive behavior pattern of "have nots." Many wealthy people have become accustomed to living high-risk lives and act irresponsibly to lose major parts of their holdings. Those who are not so wealthy have greater reasons to <u>not</u> fall into the abyss; they want to maintain a lifestyle above subsistence, one in which there is a reasonable level of comfort and hope for further prosperity.

Perhaps the most insightful book written on the Republican mind is *The Republican Brain* by Chris Mooney, currently the chief environmental reporter for the Washington Post. He had previously written a prescient book in 2007 titled *The Republican War on Science*.

What is central to virtually all writing on the Republican brain is that many Republicans seem to rely more on emotions than on reason. Some observers call it a different form of reality. Comedian Stephen Colbert simply says, "Reality has a well-known liberal bias."

Examining the Republican Brain presently is important for at least two reasons. First, over the past fifty years, conservative Republicans have moved further away from the mainstream of American political thinking. Second, during that period of time, we have opened an entirely new field of study, brain differences among people of different political persuasions.

Among the primary points that Mooney makes in his book about the differences between Republicans and Democrats are:

Republicans are less open to new ideas.

Republicans are more likely to be "authoritarians," believing in absolute truths and having confidence in leaders who purport to have absolute answers. (e.g. a Nixon, Cheney or Trump)

Liberals tend to be more open to new experiences than conservatives.

Republicans are more likely to believe in a literal interpretation of the Bible.

Republicans live in greater fear of the unknown.

Republicans are less likely to accept scientific findings if those findings run counter to their set beliefs (e.g. climate change).

Republicans in the United States are unique among political parties across the industrialized world. They are the only group that does not accept the scientific findings about climate change. Mooney writes, "At least since the time of Ronald Reagan, but arching back further, the modern American conservative movement has taken control of the Republican Party and aligned it with a key set of interest groups who have had bones to pick with various aspects of scientific reality—most notably, corporate anti-regulatory interests and religious conservatives. And so, these interests fought back against the relevant facts—and Republican leaders, dependent on their votes, joined them, making science denial an increasingly important part of the conservative and Republican political identity."

Mooney sees the rise of the Religious Right as a defense of cultural traditionalism which had been threatened by the counterculture of the 1960s, the *Roe v Wade* decision of 1973, the feminist movement and more recently the expansion of rights for those in the LGBTQ community. From the perspective of social conservatives, it is not just that these changes occurred, but that they took place so quickly.

What is clear is that if we consider the twin pillars of sound public policy to be critical thinking and empathy, the Republicans have steered away from both. It is no wonder that they are seen by many as the party of NO; opposing virtually any legislation or regulatory changes that seek to advance the public good.

But Democrats too have ways of cloistering themselves in a bubble and making themselves distant from many voters who want their leaders to be "more like them." A very astute writer about Democrats is someone who awakened many to the new Republican Party. In 2004, Thomas Frank published "What's the Matter with Kansas," a treatise on how a majority of voters in Kansas were willing to sacrifice economic gain in order to adhere to their positions on "social issues" such as abortion, gay rights, and the Second Amendment. But then he turned his focus to the left and in 2017 published "Listen Liberal" about how tone-deaf so many on the left can be.

His primary point is that the main constituency of the Democratic Party has changed since the time of the New Deal, even since the Great Society. Democrats formerly were the party of the economically deprived: those who were struggling and who benefited from legislation that gave them the right to organize and be eligible for government assistance. That help could come in the form of job training, new work opportunities, and on occasion, direct cash benefits. But in the sixties and beyond, the party changed. The metamorphosis of the party has been largely invisible to many people who call themselves steadfast Democrats.

Democrats used to consider themselves to be the party of a certain class—generally known as working class (which included both people who had jobs and who did not). According to Frank, the Democrats are now primarily the party of a different class, the professional class. Like their predecessors in the party, they show considerable concern for the interests of the social class they represent. It's just that the class they care about most is not that which was of greatest importance to Franklin Roosevelt, Harry Truman, and Lyndon Johnson, namely the economically disadvantaged and socially oppressed.

Columnist David Brooks asserts that professionals really do not think of themselves as a class; they prefer to be known as "the best." He goes on to say, "We always overlook the class interests of professionals because we have trouble thinking of professionals as a 'class' in the first place." Now he considers professionals the Democrats' favorite constituency. Between the Eisenhower era and today, professionals undertook a mass migration from the Republican to the Democratic Party.

Professionals are more than well-educated and economically well-off. By virtue of their positions, they become authorities on all sorts of issues in our society, ranging from fashion to dollars and sense to prescribing medical and legal advice. They forecast the weather, consider themselves experts on gardening, what to eat, how to exercise and even how to be at peace with yourself.

If professionals have high self-esteem, they rarely shy away from an opportunity to spread the word about who they are and with whom they are associated. Look at the letterhead of a legal firm. Check out the Board of Directors of a non-profit. Go to the symphony or a play at a theater and see how everyone is listed and ranked by how much money they give (or have to give). In the world of politics, name plastering is everywhere with endorsements and host and hostess name recognition at various events, particularly fund-raisers. In politics, "naming rights" is a key coin of the realm. Political fundraisers can list up to one hundred names as hosts and hostesses; candidates may include up to five hundred names as supporters on the digital or printed literature. The names have caché if they come from a doctor or lawyer. The names of coal miners or other blue-collar workers are unlikely to appear. Hypocrisy Alert: The testimonials that I have gathered to promote this book would seem to indicate that I am playing this very game.

All of this must look rather strange to those who are not professionals and are without significant financial means. They might envy it; they might laugh at it; they might disdain it. What the self-promotion practiced by many professionals does not do is to connect them with the traditional base of the Democratic Party.

Franks says that many professionals care little about inequality; they are more concerned about preserving their own way of life. "While this segment of the population tends to be very liberal on questions of civil liberties and sexual mores, professionals are 'not at all liberal on economic and equality-related issues.'" On anything having to do with organized labor, they are often downright conservative, preferring to maintain the *status quo* of the current hierarchy within the division of labor.

It is Franks' assertion that there is a clear dichotomy between the professional Democrats of today and the rank and file workers who were the core decades ago. As smart as the professionals are, many seem to have a blind spot as to how self-centered their agenda. Most non-professionals have gone to the Republican Party, but in 1968, Alabama Governor George Wallace attracted them to the American Independent Party and four years later he ran in the Democratic Party against eventual candidate George McGovern.

This comfortability that traditional blue-collar Democrats now have in the Republican Party was never so clear as in the 2016 presidential election. Hillary Clinton all but forgot about them and when she saw where they had gone, she called them a "basket of deplorables," hardly an endearing term designed to win votes.

A resurgence of the Democratic Party began in late 2016 after Trump was crowned king of the Electoral College. Quickly, a progressive agenda became once again acceptable. Bernie Sanders had done much to pave that road in his primary battles against Hillary Clinton.

But we all know that political preferences swing like a pendulum. The current Democratic Party is now talking more about the needs of those who struggle economically, but most Democrats still live in the world of professionals that is very distant from people in Appalachia or other areas populated primarily by economically struggling white people.

There is an obvious hypocrisy in Democrats being so attached to living the good life while expressing their concern for those in need. If Democrats really want to bring more people into the fold, get more people to engage in politics, attract more Democrats to the voting booths, they are going to have to sacrifice. It does not mean giving up more than a fair share of their wealth. What it does mean is finding more time to come down off their professional pedestals and interact with the economically less fortunate, all the while trying to keep the balance of power between them and others not so dramatically tilted in their favor. The fabric of the Democratic quilt must include virtually anyone and everyone who suffers from injustices or inefficiencies in our top-down economy. Why? Because if we are to fulfill our promise of being a real democracy, we have to take steps to ensure more equality within our society. It is also politically wise for Democrats to focus on the needs of all who are disenfranchised, regardless of their color, because that group is clearly a majority.

There was a time not too long ago when there was overlap between Republicans and Democrats and bi-partisanship existed. Republicans have moved too far to the right for compromise to be possible. But Democrats need to recognize how the bubble that they have created for themselves often precludes them reaching out to others who feel ignored by them. These people now tend to vote Republican by default. Polarization will continue unless the nature of politics drastically changes. In the short run, both political parties need to find ways to welcome political introverts into their tents. In the long run, the main change agent must be our schools.

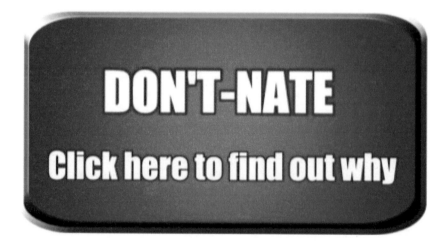

When Arthur ran for Congress in 2010 and 2014, he wanted to "walk the walk" to avoid the entanglements that occur when mixing politics and money. The image above was on his web site. As a political introvert, he truly dislikes the constant assault from politicians and political action groups asking for money.

Chapter 07

ACTIVE RATHER THAN PASSIVE MEDIA

T HE CANADIAN PHILOSOPHER Marshall McLuhan coined the phrase, "The medium is the message." What he meant is that while the content of a message is significant, the way in which it is communicated from one person to another is often more important. There is a tremendous difference between learning about a political candidate from a newspaper article and a multimedia online presentation. How our brains receive information will in part determine how we process that knowledge.

The media essentially controls how the public hears about politics. Some might like to think of the media as being a neutral force, but every action reflects one form of bias or another. In television news, we know that Fox News has a conservative bias and MSNBC's is progressive. But the real favoritism is demonstrated by what stories a media outlet chooses to cover and what specifics are presented in that coverage.

Think about the number of decisions that the producer of a half-hour television news program makes. Should she cover the crime story or the announcement by a "political maverick" that he is running for office? Should he cover the fire, or the fact that Open Secrets just revealed that one of our local members of Congress is receiving Dark Money. Should she cover the story of the woman who lost her five cats, or the story about a proposed new housing project for lower-income families that will be built in a middle-class neighborhood?

The stories to cover are the first line of decision-making. Right now, particularly on the local level, the priority is crimes and fires. "If it bleeds, it leads." National network news is trending this way as well because the ratings are good for various forms of disasters.

It's not all bleak, from time to time media outlets attempt to cover stories about how we govern ourselves. But, if a station runs a story about the political maverick announcing his candidacy for a new office, does it contain anything more than a mere mention of the announcement? If the news producer wants to be part of the public's education process, she has to do more than drop the name of the candidate and instead include details on the unique policies he is advocating. An interview with a few tough questions would also be good. How is he going to raise necessary money without becoming beholden to the donors?

Suppose that a news outlet presents a story on the Iowa Caucuses. Is the story just going to be about the horse race or the latest predictable statement by one of the candidates? Will the story include mention of the fact that while Iowa is the first contest in the road to the nomination, Iowa's caucuses include only a small portion of the state's population, and the state demographically does not look at all like America as a whole? As we said, the media is all about selection, and if outlets do not include information that is relevant to why our democracy may not be working well, then the media is missing large portions of the story. Currently, it seems that many political pundits are so excited the Iowa Caucuses are growing near that their engagement in covering the race blinds them to the absurdity of the whole event.

If the media is covering a story about how Senate Majority Leader Mitch McConnell is refusing to allow legislation regarding meaningful gun control or immigration reform to reach the floor of the Senate, will it report that there are enough Republicans who support discussion of these items to form a majority of the Senate? Will the media point out that our federal legislative body is not functioning in a democratic manner because the rules permit leaders to stymie the will of the majority? Will the media mention that both parties have favored this mal-distribution of power and that it is the American people's whose will is really stifled?

Political candidates are often asked what is the most pressing problem that America faces. Currently, there is a near-consensus it is climate change, at least among Democrats. In many ways, selecting climate change as the number one problem is a safe choice. Since 2013, the percentage of Americans who know that climate change is human-caused has jumped from forty-seven percent to sixty-two percent, though we are left scratching our heads about the other thirty-eight[22]. But rarely does a candidate point out as a major issue that the media for not giving serious consideration to public matters. It is understandable that candidates would shy away from this. They do not want to alienate the medium through which they present their message.

When I ran for Congress in 2010, the local media paid scant attention to me. While it was true that I had little chance of

---

22   https://climatecommunication.yale.edu/publications/a-growing-majority-of-americans-think-global-warming-is-happening-and-are-worried/

winning, I still was the candidate of one of our two major parties for a federal office encompassing three-quarters of a million people. My opponent was the now-infamous Todd Akin, so between the two of us, we provided a very clear choice in policy positions, human rights, and how government operates best. I received little coverage from our local daily newspaper, the St. Louis Post-Dispatch[23]. What was more distressing was how the on-line print outlet for St. Louis Public Radio preferred to spend its time chasing a fellow named Ed Martin running in another local Congressional district. Martin engaged in constant name-calling and the politics of the absurd, and St. Louis Public Radio covered whatever he did. When I ran a campaign based on elevating the conversation, I was basically ignored. Certainly, I have some sour grapes, but if the local NPR affiliate is "chasing ambulances" instead of covering proposals for fundamental changes to the ways in which we do politics, we are clearly in trouble. Their stated reasons for not covering my campaign was because "I didn't have a chance of winning." That begs the question of the self-fulfilling prophesy. If they had covered me, I certainly would have had a better chance of winning. My concern goes beyond me, it stretches to every political introvert who wants to run for office. Active media is essential to improving the quality of life in America. It needs to always be searching for candidates who bring serious ideas to the public, especially when their campaigns model a more thoughtful approach than traditional campaigns.

Fortunately, there are examples of print and broadcast media presenting articles and programs that elevate public awareness

---

23   https://www.stltoday.com/

of issues. On the national level, networks such as CNN and MSNBC have done a remarkable job of giving substantive air time to presidential candidates for 2020. Shortly after the 2016 election, Chris Hayes of MSNBC hosted a town hall in a West Virginia coal mining community with Bernie Sanders. This was an outstanding opportunity for a progressive office-holder to explain his philosophy to people who had largely voted for Trump. More than once during the televised town hall did West Virginia citizens come to see how the progressive agenda in many ways addressed their needs far better than the anger and lack of substance to the Trump philosophy.

In summer 2019, MSNBC presented a four-part series called "American Swamp." Journalists Katy Tur and Jacob Soboroff focused entirely on the way in which Americans are now "doing democracy." It is not very democratic. In the first episode, they examined the role of money in American politics. In the second, they revealed how the Trump presidency reflects the numerous conflicts of interest in American politics. The third focused on voting rights and wrongs and the final episode was called "Bill to Nowhere," describing the undemocratic fashion in which Congress operates and how stressed out members of Congress are.

This MSNBC series provided a roadmap to reform. The question now is whether MSNBC or any other media outlet will do the necessary follow-up. Are steps being taken to clean up the swamp, or is it just getting smellier?

As MSNBC and CNN continue to present substantive interviews with candidates in the 2020 cycle, voters can learn how to make assessments about thoughtful candidates. But for many voters, all of this information is fast-tracked; it's difficult to know the background to the issues which the candidates are discussing. Kati Powers, an assistant general manager at a Drury Hotel, puts it this way:

"I think that sometimes it's kind of confusing to me. I've always voted Democratic. When I was younger, I didn't really know anything about politics. I often listened to my uncle who is very largely on the other side, Republican. He and I would talk about it and he would say, "You're just saying Democratic because that's the cool thing to do. That's what all your friends are saying." And I'm like, "No." But at that time, I really wouldn't be able to talk to him about it because I didn't know as much about it as I do now. In recent years, I have been looking for my own sources of information. Now my main source is NPR. I love it so much that I became a sustaining member. I still think that much of it is confusing to fully understand."

Kati makes a really important point. How do you jump on the merry-go-round when it's already spinning quickly? If you're Kati and you really did not decide that you wanted to become engaged in politics until you were in your mid-thirties, how do you make up for all of that time lost?

No one should be prevented from pursuing a new interest, particularly one of such public importance as current events and politics, just because their interest did not pique until years later than for many others.

The solution requires some help from the media, but also all internet outlets, the publishing world, and our schools. We need a mechanism by which citizens can get objective information about current events, information that meets each individual's needs, greets them at the place where their personal continuing education needs to begin.

We have to be careful with this, because the word 'objective' has a meaning that may distort reality. Different people have different takes on objectivity. But there are outlets that have done a good job of presenting more than one side of a story. A good example is the print and digital magazine The Week.

The overall job is a task for a non-profit organization waiting to be invented. Ideally, the content would be informative like Wikipedia, but far more readable. It would have a limited scope, focusing exclusively on current events and politics. Online information would be available free of charge for anyone who wanted it and human beings would be available to provide information, context or interpretation for what was not available on-line.

This is an entirely new way in which to try to help people develop their critical thinking skills. The strength of it is that it would be independent. It would not have to fight the hurdles of bringing real critical thinking into schools or persuading the media to cover stories with facts, content and context. It would be available to students who are not finding what they need in school but want to get it. It would be ideal for people whose education has ended, or made it through school while paying little attention, or whose political growth was stunted by one or two overbearing parents.

Unlike Wikipedia, it would provide a variety of reading levels. The length of the articles would also vary depending on how much the reader wanted to take in at any given time. Graphs and charts would be user-friendly with plenty of explanation as to how to interpret them.

In the spirit of the non-profit that would provide this information, an additional positive step would be to help individual PBS stations provide their own nightly local news programs. They would not require the expense of numerous vans running all over the community to chase crimes and fires. Instead they would be designed to clearly explain issues pertinent to the community, have interviews with knowledgeable people, and take viewers on "field trips" to not just tourist venues, but to the businesses, government offices, social service agencies, etc. where the day-to-day work is done in the community.

The past forty years has seen a tremendous decline of readership of daily metropolitan newspapers. Much of this was inevitable as people often came to opt for "free" sources of news on the internet, but one of the big problems related to internet is that "fake news" keeps raising its ugly head. For people who are not good critical thinkers, trying to eliminate fake news from their feeds is somewhat like playing whack-a-mole. It's everywhere, and won't go away.

Virtually all metropolitan newspapers now have online editions. In most cases, they are more convenient than print editions. They also offer the advantage of multimedia presentations, but like the print editions, they must be self-sustaining.

The newspaper industry has faced declining revenue for years. To a large extent, both print and digital outlets receive a great deal of their revenue from advertising. As the revenue has declined, the expenses have not. It really does not matter whether a story is received by a reader in print or digital form. Behind the story, there are one or several journalists as well as editors and managers. They need to be paid; needs to have resources to cover the stories. These include transportation, equipment, fees, anything which does not come free, and that is most things.

There are models for supporting important journalism. The Pulitzer Center on Crisis Reporting is a non-profit organization that depends on donations, large and small. The mission of the Pulitzer Center is to cover international stories that are "misreported, under-reported, or not reported at all." They do an outstanding job of this.

Daily newspapers, magazines, podcasts, etc. may need to be supported in similar ways. I realize that we are calling upon resources from an already over-taxed source, the charitable instincts of the American people. Perhaps our society could find ways to redirect some money from large universities and other institutions that have far more money than they may need.

When we spoke about "The Democratic Brain," we indicated that unlike former times, the strongest constituency of the current Democratic Party is not people who are struggling economically. In fact, a plurality of modern Democrats is economically quite comfortable. Some see the wealthiest Democrats as "Limousine Liberals," living the good life while espousing the liberal agenda. Whether true or not, these wealthy Democrats give a great deal of money away to charity. Directing it towards media sources, nonprofits, and start-up schools that can promote critical thinking and empathy would have tremendous positive societal pay-offs. The media and liberals have always been good friends, now is a good time to strengthen this relationship.

Marshall McLuhan went on to say that at times the media can

be "hot" and at times it can be "cool." By hot, he meant loud, like a rock concert, a NASCAR race, or a Trump rally. By cool, he meant quieter and more thoughtful like a PBS NewsHour interview or Frontline. The word "quiet" is important. Look for books about introverts and see how many of the titles include that word. If we want to make politics more inviting for introverts, we need more political coverage to come to us through a "cool" medium. It can be over the airwaves of network or cable television, but perhaps best so over the internet where there are more choices.

A candidate like Pete Buttigieg communicates in a low-intensity fashion, one that allows the viewer to relax while listening. That is quite different from Donald Trump, but also from Bernie Sanders and Elizabeth Warren. The medium is there for the "cool" candidates to reach out to political introverts and others. What we need are more such candidates and mainstream media willing to cover them.

Chapter 08
NEEDED STRUCTURAL CHANGE

THE FOUNDING FATHERS wake up in 2017 and find out Donald Trump is president. Is this an "oh shit" moment or what? Do they ask, "Does the problem of electing the likes of Donald Trump and Richard Nixon as presidents of this country have anything to do with the decisions we made?"

The Founding Fathers inadvertently set up a system that includes considerable confusion and definite obstacles to democracy. If our contemporary goal is to make participation in our democracy more welcoming, particularly for political introverts, we must change the structure of our system. To the millions of Americans who are not political, the current arrangement is perceived as forbidding and somewhat of a closed club. Nowhere is that more evident than in the Electoral College.

Our studies have shown that one of the best ways to motivate non-voters to vote is to ensure when they cast a vote, it absolutely counts. The Electoral College muddies the waters for them, and others as well. Abolition of the Electoral College, or at least major reform of this institution, requires a concerted effort. Regrettably, those in the best positions to advocate these changes, such as our former Democratic presidents and nominees, have been largely silent.

Alexander Hamilton wrote in Federalist 68, "The process of

election affords a moral certainty, that the office of President will never fall to the lot of any man who is not in an eminent degree endowed with the requisite qualifications.[24]" Despite Hamilton's contention, we've had a handful of poor presidents in the first 190 years of the Republic. Since 1968, the situation has become alarming as our presidents have included Richard Nixon, George W. Bush and Donald Trump, three men who for various reasons never had the requisites to be president. Bush did not have the mental capacity to handle the challenges of the presidency while neither Nixon nor Trump had the psychological stability to push away personal demons and focus on the tasks at hand. It is important to note that both Bush and Trump were initially elected by the Electoral College while they had lost the popular vote by millions.

We can critique some of the choices the founders made, but considering the era in which they lived, they did an outstanding job of writing their chapter of the United States Experience. They were men (not women yet) of the Enlightenment, who valued reason and fairness. It is terribly unfair to expect that they could have predicted what the law of unintended consequences would have brought them over the next two and a half centuries. Our leaders of today seem to fall far short of the standards set by the founders.

In recent years, our democracy has not been working well. Since 1969, in seventeen of fifty years, the White House has been occupied by Nixon, G.W. Bush and Trump. That's more than one-third of the time. We're in a slump, or more likely, something has happened to the American people so that we cannot filter out unqualified individuals running for president. So, as we look to

---

24   https://avalon.law.yale.edu/18th_century/fed68.asp

change, among the challenges we face is the need to examine the structural problems that we have in our democracy and what we can do to fix them.

Structural changes are essential to engaging more political introverts into the system. The confusion of how we "do democracy" in the United States is a deterrent to involvement, just like the loud noises of many political gatherings. In many places, our system is lacking in logic and fairness. These shortcomings are a turn-off to political introverts. Reforming the inherent injustices in the Electoral College or gerrymandering is even more than many extroverts want to address. The challenges are even more forbidding to political introverts. We need a clear pathway to how democracy works in America. All of us, extroverts, ambiverts, and introverts will have to pull together on these necessary reforms.

There are several suggested reforms in this chapter. It is important to not see them as singular and isolated. They all have a common denominator: to advocate democracy where fairness is currently blocked. The principles behind abolishing the Electoral College are the same as stripping ninety-five percent of the powers of committee chairs in Congress. The idea is to get more oxygen into the system. There is no better place to start than with the Electoral College.

The Electoral College

A clear majority of Americans agree that the Electoral College is an obstacle to democracy[25]. The origin of the problem was and is the power of the individual states. A quick refresher: as the presidential

---

25 https://www.politico.com/story/2019/03/27/poll-popular-vote-electoral-college-1238346

elections are currently structured, the winner of the presidential elections is the candidate who wins the most electoral votes.

The Electoral College is a group of people that is reconstituted every four years, in presidential election years. The number of members in the "College" from each state equals the number of members it has in Congress (the sum of its representative in the House plus its two senators). The identity of the individual electors is largely unknown to the public because they are often major contributors best known to the political recipients of their largesse.

Thus, there is a certain democratic element to the Electoral College because bigger states have more electors than smaller states. But the main problem with the Electoral College is the "winner take all" feature, meaning whichever candidate gets the most (plurality) of the votes in each state gets one hundred percent of its electoral votes (**NOTE:** Two small states, Maine and Nebraska, are exceptions where each elector represents the winner of individual congressional districts rather than the state as a whole).

Here's the problem. Suppose that Candidate A wins California by a mere hundred popular votes. She then receives fifty-five electoral votes.

Candidate B wins Wyoming by one-hundred thousand popular votes and receives three electoral votes. In this scenario, Candidate A leads in the electoral college by fifty-two votes, but trails Candidate B by 99,900 popular votes. Read this again if it seems odd. Does this seem fair?

It's a joke for the United States to consider itself a democracy and for its citizens to not vote democratically (directly) for president. All other major industrialized countries in the world vote directly for their leaders.

There are two ways to get rid of the Electoral College. The first is through a constitutional amendment that would eliminate it, but progressives know when we start changing the constitution, we run the risk of conservatives wanting to take drastic actions such as making abortion or gay marriages unconstitutional and further suppressing the votes of minorities.

An easier, but less permanent way, would be through a method known as the National Popular Vote. The **National Popular Vote Interstate Compact** (**NPVIC**) is an agreement among a group of U.S. states and the District of Columbia to award all their electoral votes to whichever presidential candidate wins the <u>overall popular vote</u> in the fifty states and the District of Columbia. The compact is designed to ensure that the candidate who receives the most votes nationwide is elected president. The compact would go into effect only when that outcome is guaranteed; i.e. those states that have agreed to accept this method would not exercise this power until enough states to form a majority of the electoral votes have agreed to utilize it. As of March 2019, NPVIC has been adopted by twelve states and the District of Columbia. Together, they have 181 electoral votes, which is 33.6 percent of the Electoral College and more importantly, 67.0 percent of the 270 votes needed to win the Electoral College and give the compact legal force.

In our conversations with voters and non-voters alike, we found the presence of the Electoral College, and all the confusion associated with it, as a key reason to be cynical about politics. It also leads to widespread apathy as there is little incentive for individuals to vote in states that are primarily red or blue since the outcome of their states' elections is essentially pre-determined.

Nominee Selection

Suppose that you are a student in a political science class, and you are asked to design a system for political parties to select their nominees for president. The idea is to create a fair system that works to give all American voters who identify with your party an equal chance for input.

The system that you create begins with something called the Iowa Caucuses. You choose the thirty-first largest state in the union, one with an African-American population of three percent (compared to thirteen percent for the U.S.) and five percent Hispanic (compared to eighteen percent for the U.S.). This state's largest metropolitan area is Des Moines, the eighty-eighth largest in the country. You decide the system by which voters will indicate their preference for president will not be a primary vote, but instead something called a "caucus" that will be held at night in the dead of winter. (February 3, 2020).

In 2016, 171,517 voters attended caucuses, representing less than nine percent of those registered to vote in Iowa. Caucuses are different from primaries. In primaries, citizens go to polling places and vote. In caucuses, extremely motivated individuals attend night-time meetings in places such as schools or churches or bowling alleys, and through a complicated system determine which presidential candidate will be allocated one or several delegates from their area.

The Iowa caucuses are the first official step in the selection of party nominees. It is hard to imagine a state that is less reflective of the population of the United States than Iowa. The result here is that a state that does not come close to demographically representing the United States has an enormously disproportionate amount of power in determining who the nominees of each party will be.

After Iowa is the New Hampshire primary. The "Granite State" is the forty-first largest in the Union; and ninety-four percent white. The largest metropolitan area is Manchester-Nashua, the 130th largest in the nation. The power that New Hampshire has in determining our nominees is almost as absurd as the power of Iowa; New Hampshire's only saving grace is that it has a primary instead of a caucus. But again, it is a northern state with a selection process in the dead of winter. Is this optimizing how democracy works?

As a teacher, I have always been a soft grader because I believe in the power of extenuating circumstances and the enormous fallibility of those who grade, but I doubt that I could give a student who came up with this plan anything above a D plus. If you tried to make the system undemocratic, it would be difficult to make it less so.

The only real asset to the current system is that it allows candidates to get close to voters, especially since so much time is spent in these two states. Campaigning door-to-door in small states is called retail politics, and candidates can engage in it when there are so few voters to meet and so much time in which to meet and greet.

Under the present system many candidates feel compelled to visit all ninety-nine counties in Iowa and the additional ten in New Hampshire. Suppose they spent most of those days instead talking to voters in Los Angeles, New York, Helena, MT, and New Orleans. Wouldn't they get a more complete picture of voters' concerns?

And in a country of 327 million people, isn't it absurd to spend considerable time trying to meet voters one by one. Wouldn't it make more sense to spend that time studying issues that the president will face, visiting different locales to learn more about their labor issues, their environmental challenges, the ways in which minorities are treated? This strategy would lead to more meaningful one-to-one interactions with voters.

As bizarre as the system is, equally strange is the deafening silence from political leaders about changing it. It is understandable why candidates now running for president don't want to challenge the *status quo*, because there could be a price to pay by insulting the Iowa and New Hampshires of the world. But there are seven current well-known Democrats who either have already served as president or vice-president or run for one of those offices and are now essentially retired. Where are their voices?

I'm talking about both Bill and Hillary Clinton, Barack Obama, Jimmy Carter, Al Gore, John Kerry and Walter Mondale (I left out John Edwards for obvious reasons). All of these leaders have played the Iowa-New Hampshire game. Some fared better than others, but how well they did is not the point. None has anything to lose by taking a stand and suggesting radical reform to the way in which America political parties select their presidential nominees.

Their leadership was especially needed after the 2016 presidential election when our democracy was being challenged on many different fronts. We need nothing less than a call for comprehensive reform to all non-democratic components of our election process, and who better to lead the charge than "elder statespersons" who no longer play the game but have a stake in correcting it for all Americans.

Reformers are advocating a number of different plans including regional primaries in which the country is divided into four regions—Northeast, Midwest, West and South, which take their turns voting first, one region per month from March through June[26]. This way states of all sizes would be included in each primary and the order of the primaries would rotate from year to year.

A one-day national primary would naturally streamline the entire process but might truncate everything into too short a period.

While some good plans have already been suggested, many more could be invented if the nation put its mind to improving our country's current system. Change will require leadership and making the process more democratic will likely require action from the Democratic Party. We need the "elder statespersons" of the Party to get front and center on this reform.

Campaigns Length

As part of our structural reform, it is imperative that we drastically shorten the length of campaigns. At this point, American campaigns for president are essentially perpetual; when one election cycle ends the next one begins. Contrast this to the United Kingdom, where many elections are as short as six weeks. The obvious problems with long campaigns are the expense as well as the personal drain on the candidates. Elections would be greatly improved if the candidates were fresh, both for themselves and for the voters.

---

26   http://occasionalplanet.org/2016/11/21/presidential-primary-system-time-repeal-replace/

1-2-3 Voting / Ranked Choice Voting

There are other ways to improve the way we vote. Maine, which operates as a laboratory for democracy rather than a vehicle in the race to the bottom, offers Ranked Choice Voting (RCV), or easier to understand, 1-2-3 voting.

Imagine a candidate for whom you really want to vote. In your mind, she is far preferable to the others on the ballot., however, reality is that she isn't likely to win. Let's say that she is a candidate of the Green Party and the real contest is between the Democrat and Republican. As things stand now, if you vote for her, you are throwing your vote away (someone should have told Ralph Nader about that in the 2000 election, particularly in Florida).

So, under present rules, if you lean progressive, your options are either to "throw your vote away" and vote Green or vote for the Democrat. But with 1-2-3 voting, you can cast your ballot for your number one choice with no risk of wasting your vote. Here's how it works:

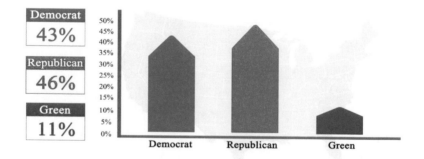

If there are three candidates on the ballot, you vote by giving each a ranking: 1 (for your first choice), 2 (for your second choice)

or 3 (for your third choice). Let's say that you give your first-choice vote to the Green Party candidate, your second-choice vote to the Democrat, and your third-choice vote to the Republican. Let's play out the scenario. After the first round of voting, the results are:

No one has a majority, but the Republican is leading. Under present voting rules, the Republican automatically wins because he has a plurality (less than a majority but more than any other candidate). However, under 1-2-3 voting rules, <u>no one wins without a majority</u>.

Under 1-2-3 voting rules, the Green Party candidate is eliminated, **but not the voters** who opted **for** the Green Party candidate. With the Green Party candidate out, the second-choice votes for the eleven percent of the voters whose first preference was the Green candidate are distributed to their second-choice candidates.

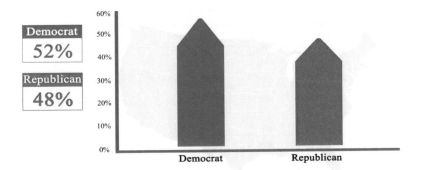

In this case, of the eleven percent Green Party votes, nine percent selected the Democratic candidate as their second choice, and two percent selected the Republican. Reallocating these votes gives updated totals of fifty-two percent for the Democrat and forty-eight percent for the Republican. The winner is determined by a majority, not a plurality, and in this case, 1-2-3 voting offers a new (and fairer) winner.

The Democrat wins and the voter who selected her first choice Green Party candidate got to cast her vote for the candidate she really wanted at no risk. With her first choice not initially winning, in the second round her vote went to her second choice. Her vote was not a throw away. She has that satisfaction, plus the additional good feeling that her Green Party candidate probably got more votes than she would have without the 1-2-3 runoff. The Green Party candidate will live to fight another battle. Maybe, in time, this candidate and others from the Green Party will become real contenders and eventually winners.

Unicameral Congress

On March 16, 2019, fifty innocent people were shot and killed in New Zealand, solely because they were Muslim. Six days later, New Zealand outlawed military-style semi-automatic and assault rifles. The ban also extends to accessories, such as bump stocks, used to convert guns into what the government called "military-style" weapons.

In the United States, we have had numerous mass killings including Columbine High School in Colorado, Marjorie Stoneman Douglas High School in Florida, Sandy Hook Elementary School in Connecticut as well as diverse venues in Orlando, Las Vegas, Annapolis and many more. Nothing has happened on the federal level, not even a ban on assault weapons or universal background checks for gun purchasers.

Here's an interesting tidbit about how New Zealand acted so

promptly to Prime Minister Jacinda Ardern's immediate call for stricter gun regulations. The legislature in New Zealand is different from America's. Instead of a Senate and a House of Representatives, New Zealand's legislature is unicameral, meaning only one house. It is more than coincidence that New Zealand's legislation could move so quickly. It's unicameral design allows for prompt, efficient changes. The United States repeatedly pays a price for a bi-cameral legislature and its built-in inefficiencies.

There are a couple of reasons why the United States has a bi-cameral legislature. The first is that the architects of the constitution were cautious about a too powerful federal government. They wanted legislation introduced in Congress to go through a rigorous process before passage. The more hoops that a bill must go through, the harder it is to pass. Passing legislation in a bi-cameral legislature is twice as difficult as in a unicameral legislature.

Competing ideas also played a role in the design of our current two-chamber legislative system. In the interest of real democracy, many of the founders of the constitution wanted Congress to be based solely on population; one person, one vote. [Keep in mind that in the 1780s a person was eligible to vote only if he was a white male who owned property.]

Remember that our constitution was assembled by men representing the thirteen original colonies. The colonies were entrenched in the political realities of the day and the founders were not going to agree to a new federal government without adequate protection for the colonies (soon-to-be states). If our Congress was solely based on population, it would favor the larger states because these states had more people and thus would have more representation in Congress. So, many states, particularly the small ones, advocated a system in which each state would have equal representation in Congress.

In our current U.S. Senate, each state has two Senators. That's the compromise that was negotiated; two houses of Congress; one based on population and the other one based on equal representation for the states. **Thus, unlike New Zealand, and fully fifty-seven percent of the countries in the world, the U.S. has a bi-cameral legislature.**

Wyoming, with a population of barely more than half a million, has two conservative Republican members in the Senate while California, with a population of nearly forty million, has two progressive Democrats in the Senate. There seems little likelihood that in either state Senatorial representation will change in the near future.

Historian Christopher R. Browning at the University of North Carolina has calculated that currently each Democratic Senator represents roughly 3.65 million people and each Republican represents roughly 2.51 million[27]. He further calculates that thirty-four Republican Senators, enough to block conviction of impeachment charges—represent states with a total of twenty-one percent of the American population. Hardly a democracy.

Anachronistic States
The current power of our fifty states in the U.S. Congress is only

---

27   https://www.nybooks.com/articles/2018/10/25/suffocation-of-democracy/https://www.nybooks.com/articles/2018/10/25/suffocation-of-democracy/

one of many ways in which states present structural problems that are counter-democratic.

In the modern world, states are artificial constructs, serving little purpose. They tend to be anachronisms, stifling the progress that a more unified government could make in addressing the needs of the populace.

Optimists like to call states "laboratories for democracy." Indeed, this does happen from time to time, particularly in "blue" states, but realists are more likely to call states vehicles for races to the bottom. The race to the bottom is competition among states to reach the lowest level of taxation and the fewest number of governmental regulations. In the vernacular, the worst insult that can be directed at a state is to call it like Mississippi or Alabama. If a state is ranked 48th in a category such as education or health care, there is a good chance that the 49th and 50th states are the two aforementioned ones. Mississippi and Alabama currently lead the race to the bottom. Ideally, they will improve, and the rising tide will lift all states.

The race is perpetually in motion. Which states can have the lowest taxes, provide the fewest services at the lowest cost, give the biggest tax-giveaways to the largest corporations? Which states can sacrifice enforcement of key civil or economic rights legislation? Which states don't mind identifying as part of the Old Confederacy and which other states don't mind keeping close company with those states in the Old Confederacy?

Let's take my home state of Missouri as an example. A good way to start is to ask a simple question. "What is a Missouri?" Think for a moment about that. "What is a Missouri?"

Missouri is nothing if not amorphous. It is designed to be dysfunctional. The state has historical significance, but when it comes to having a clear contemporary definition, or being structured to serve the needs of its people, Missouri is one big mess.

The state has two large metropolitan areas, St. Louis and Kansas City. The interests of these cities, their metropolitan areas and most importantly the people who live in them are constantly overridden by the state government in the outpost capital of Jefferson City. St. Louis recently passed a law raising the minimum wage. It costs more to live in the St. Louis metropolitan area than it does in rural Missouri, but the state government did not like the city of St. Louis acting independently, so it passed a law to disallow the increase in the minimum wage. The state prevailed.

Medicaid expansion has not happened in Missouri despite all the incentives to do so under the Affordable Care Act (Obamacare). Too many rural legislators think that funding Medicaid is a handout to lazy (and usually black) citizens living in the cities. The people's needs are not met.

St. Louis and Kansas City have problems that don't occur in metropolitan areas like Atlanta, Dallas, Denver, or Indianapolis. Both St. Louis and Kansas City's metropolitan areas crosses state lines. The St. Louis metropolitan area has a population of 2.8 million people, of which seven-hundred thousand (twenty-five percent) live in Illinois (Metro East).

Many Americans think that Kansas City is in Kansas. There is the town of Kansas City, KS with a population of 153,000. But the "main" Kansas City is in Missouri with a population of 489,000. The entire metropolitan area consists of 2.4 million, of whom forty-three percent live on the Kansas side of the border.

Constructing a regional government is much more complicated in the Missouri cities than in Atlanta, Dallas and others in which the entire metropolitan area is in one state. If states were stripped of their power, then St. Louis, Kansas City as well as countless other cities that are situated along state borders would be in positions to create metropolitan governments.

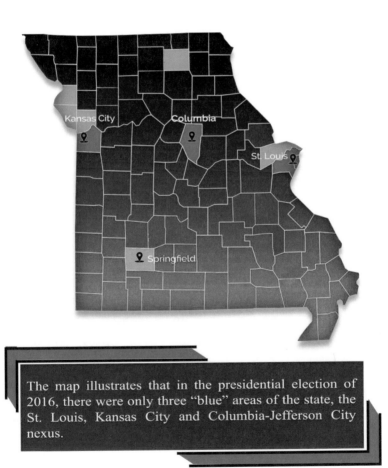

The map illustrates that in the presidential election of 2016, there were only three "blue" areas of the state, the St. Louis, Kansas City and Columbia-Jefferson City nexus.

The state of Missouri has jurisdiction over only seventy-five percent of the St. Louis metropolitan area and fifty-seven percent of the Kansas City metropolitan area. On the St. Louis side, collaboration between Missouri and Illinois governmental entities is almost non-existent and declining.

On the western side of Missouri, Missouri and Kansas cooperate a little more, in part because a river does not divide them as is the case with Missouri and Illinois (the Mississippi River).

Missouri's other metropolitan areas, Springfield and Columbia-Jefferson City, are both entirely contained within the state boundaries and distinct from the rural areas of Missouri. Springfield has a population of 462,000. Columbia-Jefferson City are thirty-one miles apart with a combined metro population of 329,000. Columbia is home to the main campus of the University of Missouri and Jefferson City is the state capital.

Missouri's political divide is illustrated by this map of the 2016 presidential election:

The question remains, "What is a Missouri?" Whatever it is, it certainly is not homogenous.

We've talked a bit about the metropolitan areas, but outside them are wide expanses of rural Midwest America. Taking another page from Thomas Frank's "What's the Matter with Kansas," the rural areas are in many ways fundamentalist in religion and conservative in politics. Collectively many love their God and guns, their autonomy, their freedom to be independent, and to see clear horizons fifteen miles in any direction.

They do not necessarily relate to the teaming stew of anger that disenfranchised African-Americans in St. Louis, Ferguson, and

Kansas City feel. They have equal trouble relating to the gentrified whites and blacks in the same communities. Their issues and concerns are largely different from those living in the metropolitan areas. Neither's concerns are better or worse, only different.

And that's the problem. Collaboration among people whose needs and concerns are so different is difficult. What is the reason why they are forced to try to collaborate under the dome in Jefferson City when common ground is scarce? The reason is because Missouri has existed as a state for nearly two centuries. Having the metropolitan and rural areas try to cooperate is like keeping an arranged marriage together when it was never designed to work. Yes, small victories happen when people with disparate priorities get along and collaborate, but by and large, our states in America represent a type of dysfunction where neither side of the cultural divide really gets what it wants.

This fragmented nature of a state is not unique to Missouri; it happens in virtually every other state.

Missouri would be a good state in which to begin reform. The goal would be this: take away those powers vested in the state that interfere with the autonomous functioning of the clearly defined regions of each state. In Missouri, clear metropolitan governments are needed for St. Louis and Kansas City. The people in the newly empowered metropolitan areas must be empowered to control their own destinies without outside interference, specifically from the state. Similarly, rural areas can flourish better when their primary focus is on those issues that are unique to where they live. Because there is more wealth in the metropolitan areas, the rural areas will be subsidized by metropolitan tax bases.

There is much internal reform that metropolitan governments must enact from within. The idea of municipalities within a metropolitan government competing with one another to give away the greatest amount of tax revenue to attract private development has to end. If a company wants to build a new corporate headquarters in the St. Louis metropolitan areas, literally more than one hundred municipalities will compete with one another to be its home. The way in which they compete is by offering tax abatements or giveaways. This is its own "race to the bottom." The solution is for each metropolitan area to have its own uniform taxing system for the entire region.

In every metropolitan area, special powers must be given so it they can govern itself. The population of metropolitan areas may be diverse, but the problems are largely homogenous. Everyone has to figure out how to get from their Point A to their Point B. Everyone needs clean air and water. Everyone needs access to affordable and quality health care. Everyone needs recreational areas. Schools are needed, available jobs must approximate the number of individuals who are looking for work at any given time.

These are problems that can be worked out locally in the individual metropolitan areas, with the help of federal resources. They don't need the distractions and clutter of state governments. We can greatly improve the quality of urban and suburban living by allowing these connected communities to govern themselves.

Similarly, rural areas do not necessarily need the "presumed wisdom," or more realistically, the economic demands of metropolitan areas. Rural areas can be designed to take advantage of their resources and the strength of the life-styles that they live.

They can enjoy accessibility to urban areas without having their way of life dominated by people who do not live, work, and worry in the same way.

Voter Suppression

As we previously mentioned, the first people who were eligible to vote in the United States were white male property owners. Andrew Jackson, who won the presidency in 1828, was one of our first populists and after losing a bizarre election in 1824 (which wound up being decided in the House of Representatives), he pushed to let white males who did <u>not</u> own property vote. He succeeded, nearly doubling the number of eligible voters.

Think of everyone who could not vote in the Jacksonian era. No women could vote. No minorities could vote. Theoretically, the 15th Amendment passed thirty-four years later in 1870 could have helped. It said, the "right of citizens of the United States to vote shall not be denied or abridged by the United States or by any state on account of race, color, or previous condition of servitude." Sounds good if you're African-American or a member of any other minority.

Here we learn an important lesson. Changing the constitution doesn't do anything unless followed by enabling legislation passed by Congress. The 15th amendment was ratified in 1870, but without federal law to enforce it; to provide penalties to those who violated it, it was essentially worthless. Not until ninety-five years later, in 1965, was a Voting Rights Act passed by Congress that put teeth into the 15th Amendment.

The Act contains numerous provisions that regulate elections. The Act's general provisions provided nationwide protections for voting rights. Section Two is a general provision that prohibits every state and local government from imposing any voting law that results in discrimination against racial or language minorities. Other general provisions specifically outlaw literacy tests and similar devices that were historically used to disenfranchise racial minorities.

Central to the effectiveness of the Voting Rights Act are the sanctions placed on states that were not permitting African-Americans to vote. In those cases, the federal government sent registrars into the states to ensure that eligible voters could both register and vote, a game-changer that soon after dramatically increased the number of African-Americans and other minorities who voted.

But forty-eight years later, one of the greatest travesties in American history occurred when the U.S. Supreme Court, under the guidance of Chief Justice John Roberts, ruled in *Shelby County v. Holder* that sufficient progress had been made to make it no longer necessary for federal registrars to be sent to the states in violation[28]. As a result of this ruling, voter suppression rebounded in the South and this virus spread to some northern states with Republican majorities in their statehouses, such as Wisconsin, Ohio, and Indiana. The Supreme Court not only took away protection for minorities in the Old Confederacy, it gave the modern Republican party in northern states opportunities to ensure its long-term presence in power through photo-ID laws and other suppressors that mainly impacted people who were poor, members of a minority, very young or very old—all people who are more likely to

---

28   https://www.brennancenter.org/legal-work/shelby-county-v-holder

vote Democratic.

As Vann R. Newkirk II reported in the Atlantic, "Journalists now commonly say that the Court "gutted" the Voting Rights Act. The more appropriate terminology might be to say that it defanged federal enforcement of that act. But looking deeper, it might be even more appropriate to say that the *Shelby County v. Holder* decision committed violence against the Fourteenth Amendment itself (equal protection under the law), of which the Voting Rights Act is a distant descendant." To ensure equal opportunities for all citizens to vote, free of voter suppression, this ruling must be overturned either by the Court itself or Congress through new legislation signed by the president.

On the positive side, the United States is about to reach its centennial of enfranchising women to vote. On August 26, 1920, the 19th Amendment to the Constitution was ratified, giving the right to vote to women. Unlike the 15th Amendment for minorities, the intent of the 19th Amendment was quickly enacted as laws were passed to ensure that women could vote. Fortunately, there are little known current efforts to disenfranchise women.

Election Security

It has been said the Russian meddling with America's elections is not necessarily for the purpose of changing results, but rather to undermine the confidence of American citizens in its democracy. As we previously mentioned, over ninety-two million eligible Americans did not vote in the presidential election of 2016. In the minds of most of these people, they have good reasons not to vote. What Russia, and possibly other countries, have been doing to interfere with America's elections, gives these non-voters further reason to take a pass on elections.

As recently as the 2012 presidential election, it would seem inconceivable to think of Russia or any other foreign country influencing American elections. Four years later, the unthinkable happened, and in ways that were unexpected and bizarre. Election officials knew of potential vulnerabilities in our electronic voting machines, especially those tied into the internet. But since 2012, considerable reform has taken place to take voting machines off-line and make it difficult for any nefarious entity, foreign or domestic, to interfere with the actual vote tabulation in an American election.

Steps taken to improve election security do not mean that attempts to interfere will not continue. The difference is that that successful meddling is less likely than earlier in the 2000s.

As we reflect upon what happened in the 2016 election, much of our focus has been on whether or not there was collusion, or even collaboration between Russia and the Donald Trump campaign. Despite extensive investigation, officials, including investigators for the Mueller Commission, have not discovered a "smoking gun" tying the two together. If cases could be made exclusively on circumstantial evidence, the existence of collusion would be a certainty, but fortunately for America, our judicial system requires proof in such cases to be "beyond a reasonable doubt."

Even without any Trump input or guidance, it is indisputable that the Russian government was working in numerous ways to affect the 2016 election. We know that they accessed voter registration rolls in both Illinois and Arizona. What we don't know is if they manipulated any of the data.

What Russia did is something that would have been impossible as recently as 2004, before Facebook was invented. Russia set up thousands of fake accounts on Facebook and other social media outlets and created ads that were pro-Trump and very anti-Hillary Clinton. Americans would go to their social media feeds and find ads that were designed to sway them towards Trump and away from Clinton. The Russians were clever with what they did and much of the messaging was very subtle. To many social media users, the impact was subconscious.

Even if the Trump campaign had nothing to do with initiating the social media manipulation, the Trump Administration and other like-minded Republicans have had everything to do with preventing adequate investigation into what Russia did. Furthermore, while other countries are taking a variety of preventive steps, the Trump Administration has drastically reduced the budget for the F.B.I. and other counter-terrorism agencies to investigate both foreign and domestic attempts to influence elections.

Since World War II, Russia and the Soviet Union have been the major threat to the United States except during the few years when Mikhail Gorbachev brought us perestroika in the late eighties and early nineties. All evidence points to Russia, China, North Korea, and a host of other countries trying to electronically infiltrate the United States. Their targets will vary from elections to the electrical grid to communication, transportation, and infrastructure. Once the nightmare of the Trump Administration is over, the government, hopefully backed by a more informed and alert populace, will move with alacrity to make up lost time and work to prevent cyber threats to our country. This is essential if we are to have hope that our democracy can function securely into the future.

Gerrymandering

Perhaps the most egregious misappropriation of power in our government is in what goes on, often behind closed doors, in our legislative bodies. In the dark to the public is how the maps are generally drawn to determine both congressional districts and those for state legislatures. Almost without exception, if a party has majorities in both houses of a state legislature and the governor is of the same party, the districts that are drawn following the decennial census will overwhelmingly favor that party. Democrats have historically been culprits of gerrymandering districts in their favor, but over the past two decades, Republicans have done so in a way that makes it nearly impossible to overturn their malfeasance.

Gerrymandering is one of the most insidious ways of undercutting democracy because it allows legislatures to shape districts in ways that favor one party over the other. Frequently, when one political party achieves a significant majority in a state legislature, the party anoints itself to draw future districts, with the intent of further strengthening its hold on the legislature.

Serious philosophical questions abound about how to draw districts. These can be challenging to the best-intentioned and fairest of determiners, but when strong party advocates take charge, any pretense of democracy can be thrown out and the results are very partisan in shape and outcome.

Let's briefly examine two ways legislators can draw districts fairly. In the first method, legislators would create districts with similar demographic characteristics to one another. Gender breakdowns, age distribution, racial differentials, income, and educational distributions would be similar in all districts. Perhaps most importantly, each district would reflect the political breakdown similar to that within that state or even the country at large. As you might imagine, that could be very difficult to do because people live

District: Texas (02)

114th Congress
Rep: Ted Poe
Party: Republican

Location

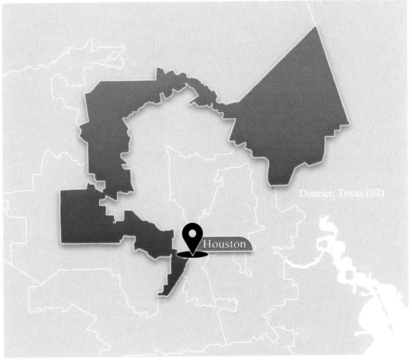

District: Texas (02)

Houston

Data Source:USGS
http://nationalmap.gov/small_scale/mid/cgd114p.html
Mapping: Alasdair Rae, University of Sheffield

in very different places, in part because they often want to be with others who are like themselves.

Take a look at the odd configuration of Texas's Second Congressional District.

Odd shapes, right? But as you know, constructing a district in Texas that reflects the state's overall demographics is difficult. These overall demographics include the following numbers about Texas:

Forty-two percent European White

Thirty-nine percent Hispanic

Thirteen percent African-American

Five percent Asian

One percent Other

Twenty-nine percent of population has a bachelor's degree or higher

Median income per household is $57,051

Fifty-one percent Republican; forty-eight percent Democrat (reflection of 2018 U.S. Senate race)

If in order to achieve this sort of equal breakdown of demographic characteristics, would it be acceptable to have such an unusual district map?

If it creates fairness, some might say yes, and they would likely expect that other "fair districts" would have similar quirky looks.

But if I told you that the district is shaped this way to keep it safe for a Republican Congressman (Ted Poe) who has been in office for fourteen years, would that be acceptable?

Imagine that you were in a circular outdoor stadium, completely full. Further imagine that you cut the stadium into four equal pieces (ouch!). That might be one way of getting fair representation, but in reality, it wouldn't because we all know some seats are positioned better than others and thus are more expensive. If there is cost variation, then there will be differences in the demographics of the people within in each section of the stadium.

Creating demographically similar districts can be difficult. So, another way in which politicians have approached districting, particularly since the Voting Rights Act of 1965, is to create "minority majority districts," areas within virtually every major metropolitan area with large concentrations of minorities. Most frequently these are African-American or Hispanic. Each of these groups have been struggling for years to get representation in legislatures. So, minority-majority districts were created.

For example, let's look at Illinois' First District.

This is an interesting district because it is represented by Bobby Rush. That name may ring a bell for you because in the 1960s he was a civil rights activist and founded the Illinois chapter of the Black Panthers. As the Panthers declined and activism moved more towards politics, he first ran for office on the Chicago City Council and in 1992 he won this Congressional seat.

Illinois-01 has been majority minority since the 1920s and Rush won in a period when the population was nearly seventy percent black. Over time, the district has become more diverse and now is only fifty-one percent black. But Rush is entrenched, the beneficiary in part of a system that provides for majority minority district. Currently, eleven percent of the members of the House of Representatives are African-America compared to thirteen percent of the entire population.

But providing majority minority districts helps Republicans as well (almost all African-Americans in Congress are Democrats). In the state of Missouri, two of eight districts are represented by Democrats; the other six by Republicans. Both Democratic districts are majority minority, represented by Lacy Clay in St. Louis and Emanuel Cleaver in Kansas City. So, in Missouri, which is eleven and a half percent African-American, twenty-five percent of its representatives in the House are African-Americans. The flip side is that the other seventy-five percent are all Republicans. Is this fair? Something to ponder.

If we were looking for Congressional districts of equal size and demographic similarity, we might try what Iowa has done, essentially dividing a small state into four quadrants.

The way Iowa draws its districts is a possible a model for the country. Rather than having the state legislature draft the maps of the districts, an advisory commission that includes specialists in

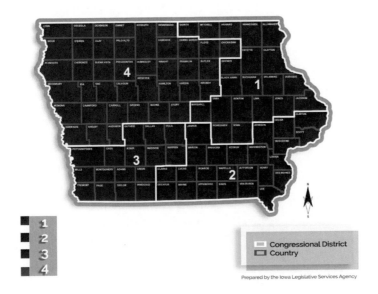

Prepared by the Iowa Legislative Services Agency

demographics creates plans which have to be ultimately ratified by the state legislature. If the districting following our last census in 2010 was random, something happened eight years later as three of the four districts are represented by Democrats and the one remaining district (4th) is represented by Republican Steve King, one of the most radical right and bizarre members of Congress. He recently said during an interview with The New York Times, "White nationalist, white supremacist, Western civilization — how did that language become offensive?[29]" He also said that abortion should be illegal in cases of rape and incest because without rape and incest, America would lose its population.

---

29   https://www.desmoinesregister.com/story/news/politics/2019/01/16/iowa-4th-district-rep-steve-king-white-supremacy-nationalism-new-york-times-racism-timeline-explain/2592434002/

Constructing fair congressional districts is difficult. In some areas, it's virtually impossible to create a similar demographic distribution within all districts. However, it is possible to try to put as many districts as possible "into play." Entrenched representatives would need to assume new risks with the possible beneficiaries being that new candidates who would now have reasonable chances of winning seats.

Clearly gerrymandering is happening on a wide-scale basis. It is a major American problem. And in June 2019, several cases related to gerrymandering were decided by the United States Supreme Court. In a decision that was as unfathomable as *Shelby County v. Holder* on voter suppression, the Court essentially punted on politically-based gerrymandering, saying they did not have a constitutional basis for intervening[30]. Chief Justice John Roberts wrote the decision regarding *Rucho v. Common* Cause and *Lamone v. Benisek*, stating, "We conclude that partisan gerrymandering claims present political questions beyond the reach of the federal courts. Federal courts have no license to reallocate political power between the two major political parties, with no plausible grant of authority in the Constitution, no legal standards to limit and direct their decisions.[31]"

There is an uncanny similarity between Roberts' thoughts on gerrymandering and voter suppression in the Shelby County case. In each, he essentially says that the Court should not be involved

---

30   https://www.brennancenter.org/legal-work/shelby-county-v-holder

31   https://www.nytimes.com/2019/06/27/us/politics/supreme-court-gerrymandering.html; https://www.washingtonpost.com/politics/courts_law/supreme-court-says-federal-courts-dont-have-a-role-in-deciding-partisan-gerrymandering-claims/2019/06/27/2fe82340-93ab-11e9-b58a-a6a9afaa0e3e_story.html

in partisan politics. That might make sense if partisan politics were not rife with discrimination, but political parties, particularly the contemporary Republican Party, discriminate through gerrymandering in a fashion similar to the ways that dozens of different kinds of oppressive laws do. Is a politically gerrymandered district no less of an infringement on a citizen's liberty than a restrictive residential covenant that does not allow him to live where he would like? Is it less discriminatory than a public park not allowing members of a particular religion to use it?

Roberts could benefit from reading Justice Potter Stewart's words in 1964 in *Jacobellis v. Ohio*[32]. The case involved obscenity and pornography. Potter said, "I shall not today attempt further to define the kinds of material I understand to be embraced within that shorthand description ["hard-core pornography"], and perhaps I could never succeed in intelligibly doing so. But *I know it when I see it*, and the motion picture involved in this case is not that.[33]"

Is John Roberts unwilling to say that he knows discrimination when he sees it, even if he cannot precisely define it? Decisions by his Court have motivated some to place on the political table suggestions to restructure the Supreme Court. This is because the current Court has undone so many tenets of our liberty and commitment to the common good.

Back to gerrymandering. Maps of congressional districts are readily available. A cursory glance can tell if one is odd-looking, or not "compact and contiguous." Rarely does a district have a bizarre shape in order to bring political balance. Frequently the bizarre shape is to promote the interests of one party or the other. What is

---

32   https://en.wikipedia.org/wiki/I_know_it_when_I_see_it
33   https://en.wikipedia.org/wiki/I_know_it_when_I_see_it

needed to make re-apportionment fair is to have people without a horse in the race do the drafting. Like so many of our political issues, we currently hit somewhat of a stone wall when we are looking for a preponderance of people who are fair and capable of making good judgments.

Organization of Legislatures

Perhaps the most invisible undemocratic component of our democracy is the way in which our legislative bodies conduct business. If you might think that the 435 members of the U.S. House of Representatives are equal in power, you would be wrong.

We should not be surprised that power is distributed unevenly in Congress because each body is made up of people who are exceptionally proficient at gaining and utilizing power and gaming the system. The problems occur when members of Congress (and state legislatures) organize themselves to do business.

Ideally, a legislative body should be like an old-fashioned New England Town Meeting in which everyone has an equal say. After all, each Member represents an equivalent part of America, about 750,000 constituents. That should be the starting point for how the House of Representatives is organized. We need to throw out the ways in which we have been doing things for centuries that exist in order to create a hierarchy of power within the legislative branch. We need to preserve and protect democracy in all possible ways within our government.

Any legislative body will need traffic cops. Why? Because each member of the legislature is trying to advance proposed legislation that he or she wants considered. Each member's bills cannot be under review or voted upon at the same time. In order to bring some degree of efficiency and specialization to the deliberations of Congress, each house has created nearly two dozen committees as well as sub-committees within each committee. Each of these units specializes in considering legislation on particular topics. For example, each house of Congress has a judiciary committee to consider the nominations for judgeships and oversight of the Department of Justice. Each house has a committee specializing in foreign affairs, national defense, transportation, the environment, education, health care, etc. This much makes sense.

The problem is when we get to the point of who runs these committees. Theoretically there could be a chairperson of a Congressional committee whose main job is to call upon each member in an orderly fashion, ensuring that everyone gets a fair chance to be heard. That's the way in which thousands, perhaps millions, of committees and boards work throughout the country.

But not so in the U.S. Congress and state legislatures. The committee chair is essentially a dictator. He or she is chosen because of being a member of the party in the majority for that particular legislative session. The Speaker of the House or Majority Leader in the Senate gets to select the chairpersons of all committees. These chairs have enormous powers. They can solely determine what issues will be studied, investigated, or under the scrutiny of oversight. The committee chair determines what witnesses will be called and whether uncooperative ones will be subpoenaed. If a chair thinks that something is not worth considering, the minority party has little or no power to address the priorities that it believes are important.

This illustrates how a change of representation in one seat can make such a dramatic difference, actually flipping control of a legislative chamber from one political party to the other. The House of Representatives has 435 members, so a majority is 218. A switch of one seat entirely changes who runs the House and how it works. If power was more equally distributed among the 435 members of the House, a change of one seat from one party to the other would have little significance.

In the Senate, the numbers are always closer. In the 115th Congress (2017-18), there were fifty-two Republicans; forty-six Democrats and two Independents who almost always voted with Democrats [Bernie Sanders of VT and Angus King of ME]. The Senate Majority Leader was Kentucky Republican Mitch McConnell who is about as cagey a person as ever held the office. After Barack Obama was elected in 2008, McConnell said that his main goal for the next session of Congress was to make Obama a one-term president. McConnell prevented considerable legislation that Democrats wanted from ever coming to the floor, in part because he didn't want them to win and in part because he did not want fellow Republicans to have to go on record as opposing popular legislation.

In the current 116th Congress, the House of Representatives has passed hundreds of bills and sent them to the Senate. Mitch McConnell does not like them, so he buries them, with no debate, much-less votes. In a truly democratic system, when the House of Representatives passed meaningful gun reform in early 2019, the bill would have gone immediately to the Senate for consideration. As Majority Leader, McConnell would have assigned it to the Judiciary Committee for hearings. Within a month, it would have been voted upon by the entire Senate. The measure might not have passed, but at least the majority will would have prevailed. There are likely enough Republicans in the Senate who favor some sort of gun control that the bill from the House, or a modified one, would have passed, but Mitch McConnell stymied the entire legislative process. It's very popular to complain about Mitch, but he's not the number one problem. It is the system by which Congress operates.

The stories are legion, but the point is simple. Our legislative bodies are not run in a way that our local Parks & Recreation Commission or high school student council is run. Congress is currently cut-throat power-grabbing. This is invisible to most of us because it is behind-closed-doors, arcane, and frankly of little interest to many voters. What's worse, it's almost a forbidden topic for the media to touch. The politicians love it that way. For us to improve our democracy, we need to elect new representatives who commit themselves to running their legislative body as a true democracy would operate.

Money & Politics

Suppose you go to a baseball game and as the managers are bringing out the starting lineups to the umpires, one of the managers gives a thick wad of cash to the home plate umpire. What would you call that? This is not a brain-teaser; you'd call it a bribe.

Now, let's suppose that a political candidate is giving a speech on a tree stump, and two voters come up to him to ask a question. One gives the candidate nothing; the other gives a wad of cash. What do we call that? Not a bribe; we call it a campaign contribution.

What's the difference? Is the voter asking for any less of a favor than the baseball manager?

Earlier, we talked about how our political system might be better if the relationship between the candidate and the voters was characterized by a more even distribution of power. Perhaps candidates and voters could relate as regular acquaintances, at least to the degree that it is very unusual for one person to ask a friend for money for personal advancement. Yes, there are times when it is necessary and appropriate to ask someone you know for money, but it is not the norm. Who would want to organize a social gathering only with friends who were sure to ask for money?

Well, believe it or not, that happens quite frequently in political campaigns with high-rollers and people of modest income. The expectation at any political event, gala to picnic, is someone is going to ask for money for a political candidate to advance his campaign. Why do you hear so many political candidates end their remarks with mention of their on-line website?

The numbers involved in political donations are astounding. According to OpenSecrets, in 2016, $6.5 billion was spent on presidential and congressional elections combined. That's enough money to build well over forty thousand dwellings for people who are homeless. It's enough to purchase nearly three-hundred thousand Toyota Priuses, something that would make our environment much cleaner.

It is not just the obscene amount of money that goes into politics, it is the source of the money. After the Supreme Court Citizens United Case of 2010, it became much easier for donors to hide behind a dark curtain of secrecy[34]. They can do this by contributing to seemingly charitable organizations called 501(c)4s, organizations

---

34   https://en.wikipedia.org/wiki/Citizens_United_v._FEC

that are allowed to donate to Political Action Committees and not reveal the individuals or corporations who are funding them. The amount of this Dark Money, so clearly and thoroughly explained by The New Yorker's Jane Mayer in 2016, is in the hundreds of millions of dollars each cycle. If you have ever heard of money from the Koch Brothers, this is how they mysteriously give.

For the sake of clarity, it is important to remember that these "nonprofits" are different from the standard 501(c)3s that are truly charitable and must reveal their donors. 501(c)3s include the Red Cross, Habitat for Humanity, Medical Students for Choice, Doctors Without Borders, etc.

We rarely know who is donating the dark money, but through reports to the Federal Elections Commission (FEC), we know the candidates who are receiving it. Candidates will not inform voters if they are receiving dark money, which is why a vigilant and responsible press is necessary to keep the public informed. Couldn't local TV stations drop crime stories for one night and reveal which candidates in their viewing area are receiving dark money?

The cost of an average campaign for Congress is approximately two million dollars. The usual cost of a Senate race is twelve million. That's a lot of money; a lot of favors to be asked. Whenever we make a large purchase, it's fair to ask, what is the ROI, return on investment?

Is a Senator who runs a twelve-million-dollar campaign one thousand times better than the candidate who runs a twelve-thousand-dollar campaign? That's unlikely. Is he or she likely to be more corruptible with the twelve-million-dollar campaign rather than the twelve-thousand-dollar campaign? Probably yes.

How much does it really cost to run a Senate campaign? Let's look back in recent history to the Senate campaigns of William Proxmire of Wisconsin.

In August 1957, Proxmire won the special election held to fill the remainder of the U.S. Senate term vacated by the death of Joseph McCarthy on May 2, 1957. After assuming his seat, Proxmire did not pay the customary tribute to his predecessor, stating instead that McCarthy was a "disgrace to Wisconsin, to the Senate, and to America."

Proxmire was reelected in 1958, 1964, 1970, 1976 and 1982. His re-elections were always achieved by wide margins, including seventy-one percent of the vote in 1970, seventy-three percent in 1976 and sixty-five percent in 1982, when he ran for a fifth six-year term.

In each of his last two campaigns, Proxmire refused contributions and spent less than two hundred dollars out of his own pocket— to cover the expenses related to filing re-election paperwork and mailing back unsolicited contributions. He was an early advocate of campaign finance reform. Throughout his Senate career, Proxmire also refused to accept reimbursements for travel expenses related to his official duties.

How's that for an honorable and effective way to deal with money in politics? Yes, Proxmire did not run two hundred dollar campaigns when he first ran for the Senate, but once he was solid, he raised zero dollars and spent two hundred, only what he needed. That's a pretty good return on investment for voters. Not only did he save campaign money, but he also created his own Golden Fleece Award in which he called out various government agencies that he saw wasting money. One of the best was a Justice Department study on why prisoners want to get out of jail.

Unlike so many of today's politicians, Proxmire was conscientious about fulfilling the requirements of his day job. He came to hold the U.S. Senate record for consecutive roll call votes cast: 10,252 between April 20, 1966 and October 18, 1988 (8,217 days without missing a vote). Compare that to many of today's members of Congress who are frequently AWOL campaigning or going to fancy events to raise big and often unnecessary bucks for their campaigns.

Proxmire's campaigns were decades before the internet. Think of how much cheaper it is to run a campaign now. Mass mailings are no longer really needed and rarely used. Phone-banking has become a better way of losing support than gaining it. It's not necessary to travel to every individual media market; one can have a remote set-up anywhere and connect with any news station.

Who has not had the feeling of saturation when watching political commercials in the weeks prior to an election? And who among us has not felt like taking a shower after being subjected to all the negative slurs cast over the airwaves? The more we pay, the more slime we get. Is that the best way to choose our leaders?

Fortunately, there are solutions to the problem of money and politics, and they can be rather simple. Instead of privately funding campaigns, the government could provide public funding. This has happened to a degree in the past and currently in the state of Maine where it is being used for a number of different offices[35]. The state of Montana has also placed very meaningful restrictions on private

---

35   https://www.mainecleanelections.org/

donations[36].

Let's suppose hypothetically that the **real cost** for an individual to run for a seat in Congress is $100,000. Let's further posit that in the average race there will be five candidates. That's $500,000. To do that in 435 Congressional races, the total cost is $217.5 million.

When it comes to the U.S. Senate, let's say that the average cost to campaign for a seat is $500,000. Let's again say that there are five candidates. That's $2.5 million per state. Only thirty-three senate seats are up at a time, so the cost for one cycle would be $16.5 million.

Let's further say that the cost of running a presidential election is $5 million and that we have thirty candidates in the running. That's a total of $150 million.

Now, the total for all federal elections in a cycle would be $384 million ($217.5 M for the House + $16.5 M for the Senate + $150 M for President).

That would be one-seventeenth of the current cost of running for federal office. This arrangement would cost about $1.16 for every individual in the United States. While it would cost the federal government approximately $333 million, think of how much money it would save because members of Congress and the president would not be beholden to any interests that were expecting financial promises for having helped put them in office.

Public financing would help clean up politics, not just because it would diminish the interlocking financial interests of politicians and people who do business with politicians, but also because it would dramatically change the nature of the interactions between

---

36   https://sosmt.gov/elections/fairelections/

those running for office and voters. As we mentioned earlier in this book, this sort of system would markedly reduce the amount of time candidates spend campaigning. That would mean more time for them to be with their families, to take walks in the park, to study the issues, to systematically prepare to do the job if elected.

This additional time would put them more on a par with the voters whom they would represent. The politicians would not spend so much time on pedestals. Also, because they would not be spending so much time with rainmakers—those who could dump large sums of money into their campaigns—they would not give a disproportionate amount of their time to people who are in what Thomas Franks called the "professional classes." He describes them as people who however well-meaning, often want to advance their personal interests through connections and networking, while not thinking much about the traditional blue-collar consistencies of the Democratic Party. In fairness, those who are struggling economically are thinking as much about their own personal advancement as the professionals when they are talking directly to the politicians, but it should be a level playing field.

Most of these structural problems have been with us since our nation was created. Bernie Sanders talks about change requiring a revolution. Similarly, if we are to reduce or eliminate the structural impediments to our democracy, we are going to need the equivalent of a revolution in the ways in which we think about how government should work.

We go back to the twin forces of empathy and critical thinking. If our schools can help future generations of adults recognize that our government needs to reflect empathy for one another and accept the value critical thinking, then we can make changes to problems such as voter suppression, gerrymandering, the gridlock of bi-cameral legislatures and uneven distribution of power among members of the legislature. We must discuss these changes now because we need a roadmap as we become more committed to making government more responsive to the real needs of the populace. These suggestions may need to be modified as we move into the era when the American people want to seriously update their government. For now, we need to clarify both our vision of and our commitment to democracy.

Chapter 9

CONCLUSIONS

O UR DEMOCRACY WILL function better if we are able to bring introverted and empathetic non-voters into the political process. These people represent a unique asset for the country—individuals who can tone down the way we do politics and elevate our conversation.

These non-voters often have good reasons to not vote such as dissatisfaction with candidates, frustration with our political system, skepticism, and yes, apathy.

Indeed, some non-voters follow the news, but generally with a jaundiced eye. They simply do not see the point in voting.

Many are open to voting if fundamental changes are made in our political process. These include:

Better, more authentic candidates—ones who are "more like them," meaning they tone down their volume, brag less and slow down their game enough to have time to listen. They also are very careful to limit the campaign donations that they receive.

Structural changes in our system— specifically with the Electoral College. No other industrialized democracy has such an obstacle to the direct election of its leaders. The Electoral College is the poster child for why so many non-voters think voting is not worth the effort.

The availability of clear and concise information about

candidates and issues—this information will have to come from a newly-created authority which earns credibility for being unbiased. It will need to provide a variety of forms of information in order to be attractive to the maximum number of current non-voters.

If we want the arc of change to move in the direction of a more informed, engaged and responsible electorate, we are going to have to dramatically change the ways in which we "do schools" in America. We have to move away from rote learning and curricula that is forced upon teachers by an often-distant bureaucracy whose main concern is self-perpetuation.

We need to open teaching to young idealists who see schools as a key place to effect societal change—to make our children and ultimately our adults more empathetic, more caring, more concerned with the common good. These new teachers will not so much teach empathy; they will model it. They will encourage students to learn more by exploration and experience. They will help students develop the essential skills of critical thinking. They will make school as fun and engaging as school can be.

Ideally students will mature into adults who are committed to bringing positive change to our political processes. They will broaden the universe of voters who see politics as a way of affecting positive change for our society, particularly for those who have historically and currently received the short end of the stick.

None of this will be easy or quick. It will take years to eliminate the Electoral College and generations to change our educational system so that we are consistently raising young people to become active, intelligent, and empathetic citizens. The prime leaders in this movement need to be current progressives, the ones who want to address disparities of wealth and human rights in this country. They need to be increasingly joined by introverts who have been dissatisfied with American politics but who will become progressively active as candidates become more real and structural changes begin to take place.

This journey is not for those who only seek immediate results and quick feedback. It is for those who have a vision of how democracy in the United States can go hand-in-hand with improving the quality of life for its citizens. A call to action would be inappropriate, because so many introverts prefer to make personal decisions without outside pressure. But if you believe the ideas in this book can help improve our politics and our country, please think about how you can play a part in bringing about the needed change.

INDEX

160 *Political Introverts*

ACKNOWLEDGEMENTS

I TRIED TO START this book but writer's block repeatedly reared its ugly head. Fortunately, I had connected with two outstanding developmental editors in Chicago, Sara Connell, and Mary Balice Nelligan. After a three-hour work session, I had the direction which had been missing. From that time on, Sara and Mary provided me with the support and guidance that kept me on track. If this book flows smoothly, give credit to them, where it belongs. My life is greatly enriched for having met Sara and Mary.

It has been a pleasure to work with Kelly Santaguida at Gatekeeper Press who took me through the difficult path running from plain manuscript to published book. Working on the cover design was a pleasure with Joshua Kaplan, an amazing artist who is very client-centered.

Mega-thanks to Elisabeth Durkin who produced the animation that accompanies this book. And thanks to Mathilde Dratwa for recommending Elisabeth.

I have been fortunate to have a terrific group of colleagues, both students and adults, with whom I have been able to discuss so many of the issues in this book. Special thanks to Bobbi Kennedy and Bill Kesler of our Occasional Planet blog group as well as Civitas summer student interns in 2018 and 2019: Katie Barefield, Lonita Benson, Reece Ellis, Maggie Hannick, Gabe Lepak, Sophie Lodes, Daria Nastasia, Jade Nguyen, Isabella Reed, Emily Scott, Claire Shackleford, Addison Steinbach, Claire Stolze, Riley Weber, Alex

Williams and Stephanie Gavin of our staff.

Also great thanks to the students and teachers at Crossroads School where I think that we learned and had fun doing so.

To our "Turkey Day" group that had a touch football game for fifty years on the Friday after Thanksgiving, thanks for all combined with great conversation about the state of the world, and gossip.

Finally, my wife, Gloria Bilchik, with whom I have had thousands of lively conversations about all topics within the book. We're news junkies. The trick is to embrace the good ideas and to privately mock the sea of b.s. in which we live. We challenge one another without acrimony. Do I really appreciate that! Thanks, GG!